"Within these pages, James Robison unpacks his journey as an invitation to each reader to see what God can do with any willing life. To me, *Living Amazed* is memoir-meets-minister. James simply cannot help helping people. It's the way God remade him in Christ. He sees no benefit in telling his story if there's nothing in it to help ours. That's what I love most about him. This I can testify as an eyewitness: James Robison has lived amazed. We can too."

—**Beth Moore**, *New York Times* bestselling author
and Bible teacher

"We've spent considerable time with James Robison over the years—on the mission field, in the *LIFE Today* studio, and in his home. We live amazed at how God has used him for decades to be salt and light to people who are hungry for the gospel. The stories in these pages will awaken something within you—a desire to make a difference in the world around you."

—**John and Lisa Bevere**, Messenger International

"James's life has had such a profound influence on Gateway Church, as well as on my life and who I am today. As you'll read in *Living Amazed*, many of the people he's influenced didn't even know he was a preacher, yet he was able to lead them to Christ. God is an amazing God and desires His amazing kids to live an amazing life, and James clearly shows us how to do that. I believe this book has the potential to change your life."

—**Robert Morris**, founding senior pastor of Gateway Church
and bestselling author of *The Blessed Life*,
Truly Free, and *Frequency*

"James Robison has hit a homerun with *Living Amazed*. Chapter after chapter of intriguing stories, and I'm amazed to see how God has used him and his wife, Betty. His boldness should be an inspiration to us all that we have nothing to fear when living for Jesus Christ."

—**Andy Pettitte**, former MLB pitcher
for the New York Yankees and Houston Astros

"I have known James Robison for half a century. These wonderful remembrances of God's amazing grace in his life will inspire anyone who reads this remarkable story."

—**Dr. Richard Land**, president of Southern Evangelical Seminary

"My dear friend James Robison has combined the truths in Scripture with real-life examples that will touch your very soul. His transparency in each story allows you a glimpse into all that is possible for one who is fully devoted to Christ."

—**Jentezen Franklin**, senior pastor of Free Chapel
and *New York Times* bestselling author

"For anyone who has ever felt spiritually unusable, burned out, overwhelmed, or overlooked, *please* read this book. You will find yourself again through these pages, and your spirit will come alive again. I was inspired through countless stories, in ways I haven't felt in a long time. God still longs to do mighty and amazing things with our lives that will accomplish His purpose and plan for each of us. Look for Him. Be available. Be willing. Be amazed!"

—**Tammy Trent**, author of *Learning to Breathe Again*

"James Robison is a big man in love with a big God by whose grace he has lived a big life. This book and Robison's amazing stories will bless, inspire, and encourage you to live boldly and enjoy the ride!"

—**Mark Rutland**, PhD, president of Global Servants

"James has touched the lives of millions in a positive way, and *Living Amazed* is an account of how and why it happened. Absolutely inspirational! A must-read for everyone."

—**David Glass**, former president and CEO of Wal-Mart

"James Robison is the most lucid and forceful speaker I have ever known. He is also one of the most balanced and loving leaders I have ever met in the church over the past thirty years. His testimony is a truth-tale of God's sovereign work in bringing a boy out of a ruinous past—and then, by God's power, raising up a man who would bring hope, health, healing, and the workings of God's hand through him into play wherever he goes. His is a story of sovereign grace, achieving sovereign works through a lifestyle submitted to the sovereign rule of Almighty God."

—**Jack Hayford**, chancellor of The King's University

"While in seminary, I studied every evangelist from the New Testament to the present day for my dissertation. One remarkable achievement I discovered was that James Robison had preached to more people face-to-face by the age of thirty than any other evangelist in all of history! It is my prayer that through the pages of this book, you get a better look at the man I have come to love and respect as one of the greatest Christian leaders of all time."

—**Frank Harber**, PhD, Southwestern Baptist Theological Seminary and JD, Texas A&M School of Law

"James Robison is a guy whose message captures the attention and love of anyone who has a heartbeat. His book *Living Amazed* is a personal tribute to the God who called James to an unexpectedly enormous, worldwide ministry. As he shares his story, you will laugh, think, and cry, realizing Jesus is indeed in all things."

—**Marilyn Meberg**, author, Women of Faith speaker, and Bible teacher

"I have known James Robison more than fifty years . . . even having the privilege to serve as best man in his wedding. His commitment to his calling has never wavered, and he is still going strong. When James speaks, you hear his heart and you are moved as the Holy Spirit speaks to you. You will be moved in the same way as you read the pages of this book. Get ready to be blessed!"

—**Dr. Billy C. Foote**, evangelist

"*Living Amazed* will help you see life differently. I have known James Robison for more than thirty years, and he has lived an amazing life . . . sharing Christ all over the world to anyone who will listen—on television, in stadiums, and in convenience store parking lots. Sharing Christ is his passion. James has inspired me, and the insights he shares in this book will capture the attention of anyone wanting to live amazed!"

—**Michael Ellison**, founder and president
of Ellison Media Company

"I met James Robison in 1966 when we were both college students. I was amazed at his confidence in God, especially considering the circumstances of his childhood. To anyone paying attention, his life obviously reflects the amazing grace of our God who works things according to the counsel of His own will."

—**Dudley Hall**, president of Kerygma Ventures
and consultant and contributor to Stream.org

"Of the many superlatives we could use to describe what marks and characterizes James's life, the most fitting is the one most people might least expect—love. Overwhelming, life-changing love. It is the radical stuff that transforms the giver and the receiver. It begins with the love of God shed abroad in our hearts, but it never ends. Just like James's Spirit-led encounter with a group of young people whose friend had died in an accident, which is described in the book, it ripples through life, leaving the unmistakable print of the finger of God on everyone it touches. This book is an unexpected encounter with Jesus, in all His mystery, wonder, beauty, and love."

—**Bishop E. W. Jackson**, founder and President of STAND
(Staying True to America's National Destiny)

"I have known James and Betty for almost twenty-five years. His life—his story—continues to inspire me. He is one of the most authentic and honest men I've ever known and, oh, how he loves. These pages not only tell a story of a remarkable life . . . but this also is an amazing blueprint to use to navigate my own path and circumstances as I learn more and more how to live and love like James Robison."

—**Chonda Pierce**, comedian, author, recording artist

LIVING
AMAZED

HOW DIVINE ENCOUNTERS CAN CHANGE YOUR LIFE

JAMES
ROBISON

Revell

a division of Baker Publishing Group
Grand Rapids, Michigan

Published by Revell
a division of Baker Publishing Group
P.O. Box 6287, Grand Rapids, MI 49516-6287
www.revellbooks.com

Printed in the United States of America

Library of Congress Cataloging-in-Publication Data is on file at the Library of Congress, Washington, DC.

ISBN 978-0-8007-2792-5

Published in association with the literary agency of The Fedd Agency, Inc., P.O. Box 341973, Austin, TX 78734.

17 18 19 20 21 22 23   7 6 5 4 3 2 1

This book is dedicated to our precious daughter

ROBIN ROBISON TURNER,

who lived for Jesus with all of her heart
and went to live with Him after a seven-year battle
with cancer on December 28, 2012.
She revealed clearly to everyone what
Jesus meant by "abundant life."

From the time she was diagnosed with throat cancer,
she signed every email to her mother and me: "I WIN."
Indeed, she has because her Savior has never lost a battle.

Betty and I recognize that Robin didn't get to finish her life
the way we all envisioned, but she did faithfully run the race,
finish the course—and she did win!
Robin is free of pain, whole, and in perfect peace forever.

What a daughter, wife, mother, sister, and faithful witness
she was during her forty-year journey
on this earth. She was truly a bright light in a dark world.
There is no doubt she lived amazed.

Contents

1

Miracle in Marble Falls

When Jesus had finished these words, the crowds were
amazed at His teaching; for He was teaching them as
one having authority.

Matthew 7:28–29

EVERYWHERE JESUS WENT during His time on earth, people
were amazed by what He did and what He said.[1] They were
amazed by His wisdom and teaching. They were amazed by
His authority over nature, illness, and demons. And they were
amazed by His miraculous healing power. Sometimes, people
were amazed simply by His presence.[2]

Even more astonishing, Jesus told His disciples that "anyone
who believes in me will do the same works I have done, and even
greater works, because I am going to be with the Father."[3] And
after Pentecost, wonder and amazement spread across the world
as followers of Jesus, living in the power of the Holy Spirit, began
to do marvelous works, just as He had predicted.[4]

But why would God use imperfect people to accomplish His
perfect will? The best explanation I've found is the one offered

by Paul in 2 Corinthians 4:7: "We have this treasure in earthen vessels, *so that the surpassing greatness of the power will be of God and not from ourselves.*"[5] Whether or not we can fully explain it, that's the way God designed it. Throughout the Bible and down through the ages, He has used flawed, weak, and wayward people to pour out His power and accomplish His purpose on the earth.

I believe that God has a purpose and a plan for *everyone.* The body of Christ contains no small, unimportant, or insignificant members.

Everyone can succeed at *serving the Lord.*

Everyone can succeed at *loving others.*

Everyone can succeed at *walking by faith, not by sight.*

The Holy Spirit can empower every believer to see the world through the eyes of Jesus and identify with the heart of God. If we show the world the loving heart of God, we will find ourselves living amazed—and God will continue to amaze us. All it takes is a little faith, hope, and trust to see the powerful hand of God at work in the world.

> If we show the world the loving heart of God, we will find ourselves living amazed—and God will continue to amaze us.

Living Amazed is all about how God will use any available instrument, any yielded life that is open to Him. If we submit ourselves to Him, there is no limit to what He can accomplish through us. God can reach people in ways that are truly beyond our imagination but completely within the realm of possibility when we allow Him to do His work through us. In fact, living amazed can begin with something as simple and ordinary as a conversation in a convenience store parking lot.

When Betty and I had been married about six or seven years, we leased a hunting property with some friends about sixty miles northwest of Austin, Texas. We planned to use it as a retreat from the pace and pressures of my preaching ministry, which at the time had me on the road more than 275 days a year.

That summer, we drove up to see the property and do some maintenance work. We took along our daughter Rhonda, who was four or five years old, and my former foster parents, the Rev. and Mrs. Hale, who were excited about getting out into a part of the state where they could see some wildlife.

After a full day of work in the hot Texas sun, we still had a four-hour drive ahead of us to get back home to the Fort Worth area, and by then evening had fallen. As we drove through a little town called Marble Falls, I said to Betty, "I gotta have some chocolate milk."

"Chocolate milk?" she said. "It's too hot out here, and I don't even think that's good for you. Let's just stop at a hamburger place and get you something to drink."

I was still sweaty from the work, I hadn't shaved in a couple of days, and I was dressed in coveralls and boots, but I had a craving for chocolate milk. That wasn't something you could get at a fast food place in those days, so we pulled in to a local quick-stop market along the way.

As I got out of the car, I noticed about thirty or forty high school–age kids hanging around in small groups in the parking lot. Some had their heads down, and I sensed they were troubled about something.

Inside the store, I passed a couple of girls who were wiping tears from their eyes, and as I made my way back toward the dairy case, I saw two more girls in the aisle who also appeared to be crying. I sensed the Holy Spirit saying to me, *James, you need to talk to these kids.*

When I got to the checkout, I said to the woman behind the counter, "I've seen some folks who are crying. What's going on here?"

"These kids are really, really sad," she said. "One of the most popular students at the high school, one of the football players, was in a car accident and broke his neck. The kids were all up here throughout the day praying that he would get well and be healed, but they just got word that he died."

Again, I sensed the Holy Spirit say, *Go talk to those boys and girls. They need to hear how much Jesus loves them.* The message was as clear to me as if it had been audible.

Here's a good example of how the enemy gets in and tries to distract us. No sooner had I heard the Lord speak than a second voice—my own voice—began to enumerate all the reasons why talking to those kids was not a good idea.

> When the enemy goes to work on us, it's not like Cupid shooting arrows of love. He fires suggestions, doubts, and distractions. But when God speaks, He speaks the truth.

You need to look out for your family, James. You still have a four-hour drive ahead of you. Betty's tired, Rhonda's tired, the Hales are tired. You're wearing coveralls, and you haven't showered or shaved. And besides, those kids are scattered all over the place out there. How would you even get them together to talk to them?

When the enemy goes to work on us, it's not like Cupid shooting arrows of love. He fires suggestions, doubts, and distractions. But when God speaks, He speaks the truth.

James, those kids need to hear how much I love them.

I paid for my chocolate milk and walked toward the exit. As soon as I touched the door handle, I saw all the kids in the parking lot suddenly come together in a circle right out front.

Okay, Lord, that's just too obvious.

In my dirty coveralls, unshaven, and looking like a bum, I stepped into the middle of the circle, looked around at all the grieving faces, and said, "Excuse me, I was just passing through town, and the lady inside told me you lost a friend. I'm so sorry to hear that. But I feel impressed to tell you that if your friend was a Christian, he's in heaven right now, and he's looking down at you and saying, 'Whatever you do, don't miss this! Don't miss heaven.' And he wants you to know that Jesus is the way to heaven.

"Now, if your friend was not a Christian, he's saying, 'I don't want you to come to where I am right now.' And if you yourself are a Christian, he's saying, 'Why didn't you tell me about Jesus? Why didn't you tell me so I didn't end up here?'

"If you didn't tell him about Jesus, you have to honestly ask yourself *why*. And if you know Jesus, you need to understand that your friends here could leave at any moment, like this boy did, and you need to be a witness.

"Those of you who don't know Christ, your friend wants to make sure that *you* don't miss heaven."

I concluded by saying, "Whatever you might think about what I just said, remember this: on the day your friend died, a stranger who was just driving through town stopped long enough to point you to Jesus and recommend Jesus to you."

Then I walked back to the van, got in, and we resumed our drive home.

That sounds like the end of the story, right? I hadn't told the kids my name, where I was from, or what I did. Nothing.

Several weeks later, we were doing an area-wide crusade in Austin. That was the crusade where eleven members of the 1969 national champion Texas Longhorn football team came to Christ, including quarterback James Street and receiver Randy Peschel, who would later connect on an amazing fourth-down pass to set up the winning touchdown against Arkansas that sealed the national championship.

After the service one night, several high school kids came up to me and said, "Sir, you're him. You don't look like him, but you're him. You're the one."

"I'm the one who what?"

"The one who stopped in the parking lot and told us about Jesus. Sir, that changed our lives."

One of the girls started crying and said, "My dad was an alcoholic, and I went home and led him to the Lord. He was killed just a short time later, but he went to heaven because you stopped at that store."

"That's amazing!" I said.

But the story doesn't end there.

Later that fall, Betty and I went up to the retreat property again. We were sitting out back enjoying the scenery one afternoon when a man in a suit and tie came walking up through the brush. He must have climbed over a barbed wire fence to get in to the property, because the gate out at the road was locked. But there he was.

He introduced himself as Max Copeland and said, "I know this may sound crazy to you, but I'm the pastor of First Baptist Church, Marble Falls, and a few months ago we lost one of our football players. The day he died, every kid in my church who could get ahold of me called to say they weren't coming back to church anymore, because they had been praying for God to save their friend's life, and he had died. I mean, their faith was totally devastated.

"But the following Sunday, they were all there in the pews, and they told me about a man who had stopped at the convenience store and shared Jesus with them.

"James, I want you to know that I baptized twenty young people who accepted Christ in that parking lot after you left. Other kids who had pulled away from God are now all on fire for Him. We are experiencing a revival in our town because of this."

"That is truly amazing," I said.

"I wonder if you'd be willing to come back and preach to us sometime," the pastor said.

I told him we were planning to come back and do some hunting soon.

"We have a big barn out in the country where folks could gather. Would you be willing to preach in a barn?"

"I'll preach anywhere."

After agreeing that Betty and I would come, I asked him, "How did these kids know who I was? I never told them."

"I put up a poster about a revival in Austin, in case some of our people wanted to go. The kids saw it and came into my office and said, 'You see that man in the picture on the poster? He's the one who stopped and talked to us in the parking lot.'"

Some of those young people were the ones who had spoken to me at the revival.

When Betty and I went back to Marble Falls in December, we drove outside of town about fifteen miles, along some country roads, until we found the barn. When we arrived, there were cars everywhere and a thousand people inside the barn. The population of Marble Falls at the time was only about fifteen hundred, but a thousand of them had come to hear me preach.

When I gave the invitation that night, ninety-nine people came forward to receive Christ. I remember the exact number because Betty and I were laughing in the car afterward that I almost asked *her* to come forward so we could get an even hundred.

Brother Max invited us back again the next summer, and we did a three-night crusade at the high school football stadium, where another 176 people made the decision to accept Christ. Out of that parking lot conversation with thirty or forty high school kids, 275 people had now come to Christ.

But the story doesn't end there.

A few years later, at a crusade in Orlando, Florida, a woman approached me after one of the meetings and told me that her daughter had been at that convenience store parking lot in Marble Falls. She had not been a Christian at the time, but with everything that happened afterward, she had come to Christ and had become a beautiful witness for Him. Recently, though, she had been killed in an automobile accident. Although the mother was grieving her loss, she wanted to thank me because she knew that her daughter was in heaven, and she knew that the turning point had been that night outside the market.

When I stopped at the convenience store for chocolate milk that evening, I had no idea what I would find there. And the kids to whom I had spoken had no idea who I was. They didn't know I was a preacher. I was just some guy who looked like a bum and had a heart for the Lord. And when the Holy Spirit spoke to me and told me what I needed to say to those grieving kids, I had all the usual excuses lined up and ready to go.

It's late. I'm tired. My family's tired. I'm busy. I need to get home. And even if I could get those kids together long enough to talk with them, why would they listen to me anyway?

But here's the point of all this: What I did that night could have been done by *anyone with a heart yielded to God*. All it took was being available, being willing, and being obedient to the call. And the result was living amazed.

Early in 2015, I called the church in Marble Falls to see if Brother Max was still around. Indeed, he was, as pastor emeritus. It had been almost fifty years, but he still remembered me. He said he would never forget the day he climbed over a barbed wire fence to come find me, because a brief encounter at a convenience store parking lot had turned his entire town inside out. That's what living amazed is all about.

Just a few months after I last spoke to him, Max Copeland went to be with the Lord at the age of eighty-five, after sixty-nine years of ministry, including fifty-seven years in Marble Falls. What distinguished his ministry in the minds of all who knew him was his genuine, steadfast love for other people. That's something we all can emulate.

What the Bible Says about
LIVING AMAZED

After the demon was cast out, the mute man spoke; and the crowds were amazed.

Matthew 9:33

Now as they observed the confidence of Peter and John and understood that they were uneducated and untrained men, they were amazed, and began to recognize them as having been with Jesus.

Acts 4:13

2

Plucked from Obscurity

All spoke well of him and were amazed at the gracious
words that came from his lips. "Isn't this Joseph's
son?" they asked.

Luke 4:22 NIV

IT'S A MIRACLE I was ever born. In fact, if the laws we have today
were in effect back then, I'm 99.99 percent certain I would have
been aborted.

My mother worked as a practical nurse, giving hospice care
to homebound individuals. She had been married at a young
age, but by the time she was forty, she was long divorced and
working in the home of an elderly man in Houston. That man
had an alcoholic son, about ten years younger than my mother,
who one day forced himself on her and raped her.

My mother lacked the wherewithal to press charges, and when
she became pregnant as a result of the assault, she went to get an
abortion, for all the reasons you would hear today—product of
rape, no father or family in the picture, mother living in poverty
and unable to care for the child. But when she went in to see
the doctor, he refused to perform the abortion.

I don't know why. Did he see possibilities and potential in that unborn child? Or did he simply believe that all life is precious? Whatever the reason, and whatever you might think about it, he refused to perform the abortion.

When I was old enough to understand, my mother told me the circumstances of my birth and that the Lord had told her, "Have this baby; it will bring joy to the world."

As a result, my mother was convinced that I would be a girl, and she was going to name me Joy. In the delivery room, when the doctor told her she had a little boy, she said, "No, I have a little girl and her name is Joy."

"You can call him anything you want," the doctor replied, "but you've got a boy."

Years later, when I met Johnny Cash, who had recorded the song "A Boy Named Sue," about a boy who was given a girl's name and had grown up without a father, I knew I had met a kindred spirit. And I was grateful that my mother had changed my name from Joy to James.

I was born in the charity ward at the hospital, and my mother immediately placed a newspaper ad seeking foster care for me. This was 1943. Doyle and Katie Hale, a Baptist pastor and his wife from the nearby town of Pasadena, Texas, responded to the ad and took me in. They raised me for the first five years of my life and were hoping to adopt me. In fact, at one time they had the paperwork drawn up, but my mother would never sign it.

When I was five, my mother showed up one day and announced that she was moving from Houston up to Austin and that I was going with her. I clearly remember running away from her and crawling under the pastor's bed. And I can remember my fingernails dragging across the hardwood floor as my mother dragged me out from under the bed by my foot. I remember that desperate clawing like it was yesterday. It was quite traumatic.

Mrs. Hale was crying so hard that she was convulsing. She had to go lie down. And Brother Hale was saying to my mother, "Please don't do this, Myra. Don't do this."

But my mother insisted. "No, we're going."

Brother Hale tried to give her a handful of money to help her out, but she wouldn't take it.

"We'll be all right," she said.

But the fact was, she had only enough money for us to get on a bus in Pasadena, on the southeast side of Houston, and ride to somewhere just on the other side of the city. That's where we got off and hitchhiked the 165 miles or so to Austin. I clearly remember sitting on a little cardboard suitcase with all my belongings in it, and my mother had a bag. I still have that little beat-up suitcase in my office today.

When we got to Austin, we moved in with one of my aunts, and my mother began looking for work. When she found a job, she needed something for me to do during the day, so when school started, my aunt, who was a teacher, paid for me to go to a private school. I was only five, but I went into the first grade and got a pretty good kick start on my education. All the way through, then, I was a year younger than everyone else in my class.

Though school always came easy to me—boringly easy—I was so shy and so afraid of everyone during my childhood that I would not even stand up in front of a class to give a report. For the first ten years of school, I was so withdrawn that I wouldn't mingle with the other kids. I carried a brown bag lunch every day, and I ate alone. When they picked teams in gym, I was the kid who was never chosen—because nobody knew me. My mother and I moved so often that I was always the new kid.

We lived in Austin for the next ten years, and over that time, we moved so often—fifteen or sixteen times—that the words *home* and *family* were meaningless to me. Most of the places we lived did not face a street or have a street address, and we would get our mail at someone else's house. I've said that our only address during those years was an alley, a creek, or a dump. If it had an address at all, it would be some number and a half. They were typically little one-room houses with the living area and kitchen all together or a little rectangular room with a bathroom attached to it. We lived the longest in the back of a junkyard, with auto parts, wrecks, and other debris lying around. That was the yard I played in.

In junior high, I walked three miles each way to school every day because my mother didn't have a car and no school bus ran by our house. During the entire ten years I lived in Austin, we never once had a car. And nobody around us had a car. So I walked.

To the Least of These

Several years ago, I was at a luncheon in Charlotte with a group of business leaders. Cathy Hendrick, of the Hendrick Motorsports family, was sharing with us at the table about a trip she had made with our LIFE Outreach mission team to India, where it was like stepping onto the set of the Academy Award–winning movie *Slumdog Millionaire*.

If you've seen the film, you know that it portrays a group of children who have been taken captive and forced to beg on the streets of Mumbai—enriching their captors while the children themselves live in poverty. Some were blinded or had their fingers or a hand cut off to make them more effective beggars. But the kids Cathy saw on the streets of India were not movie actors, and the suffering was real.

She told of how our mission team went to these children and loved them and cared for them in our LIFE Centers, which are homes we have established in nations around the world to provide a loving atmosphere, food and clothing, a safe place to sleep, an education, and godly instruction for kids in need. And then she said, "I just watched these little kids who were staring at our team, and we would talk to them, and they would say that somebody had left them and they didn't know if they were ever coming back."

When she said that, I broke down and wept at the head table. I cried so hard that I had to lay my head down on the table. You see, I flashed back to the first five years of my life, when my mother would come and get me at the Hales' when I was three or four years old, and she would take me with her for three or four days at a time, but then she would leave me at somebody's house because she would have to work and couldn't take me with her into the homes of her patients.

The people she would leave me with were always really nice to me, and they would say, "Hey, James, here's your room, if you want to go into your room." But I can remember just going to the front window and putting my nose up against the glass or the screen, staring outside for hours, wondering if my mother was coming back to get me. Those times gave me a real feeling of being overlooked—and it hit me like a ton of bricks when Cathy Hendrick shared her experiences in India.

I think that's why, when I read my Bible, I have such a tender heart for King David.

David was a kid who, in the eyes of his own family, didn't seem very significant. When Samuel came to anoint the next king of Israel from among the sons of Jesse, Jesse didn't even think to call his youngest son in for consideration. But David was faithful in taking care of the sheep. He loved and protected them. Toiling in obscurity while his older brothers were off serving in King Saul's army, David killed a lion and a bear to protect his sheep. And one day, in the same confidence, he would kill the enemy of God's people.

David lived amazed, and God did amazing things in and through his life. He wasn't perfect. His failures were epic and legendary. But in the balance, he became known as a man after God's own heart.[1] Even in his darkest days, he couldn't stand to be away from the presence of his heavenly Father. He not only *lived* amazed, but he showed the world amazing grace and a brief glimpse of the King of Kings and Lord of Lords.

> David lived amazed, and God did amazing things in and through his life. He wasn't perfect. His failures were epic and legendary. But in the balance, he became known as a man after God's own heart.

When looking at David's exploits, it's easy to forget that he wasn't born into privilege; he was plucked from obscurity. And yet God used him mightily. And God can do the same with you and me—if we're faithful while tending the sheep and not being noticed; if we love the Father; and if we love the family of God, even when they don't notice us and don't think we have any ability; and even if we're young, shy, and scared.

I think also of Gideon, whom the Bible describes as the least of the least—not because he was insignificant, but because he *felt* that way. But God had big plans for Gideon, and all Gideon had to do was respond in faith and obedience.[2] How would you like to put to flight an army with soldiers "as numerous as locusts" and camels "as numerous as the sand on the seashore," and do it with only three hundred soldiers of your own?[3] That's the equivalent of an average-size church congregation in America today taking victory over enemies beyond number. That's what living amazed is all about.

Those years that I lived with my mother allowed me to see the reality of people's pain. Today, whenever I see an overlooked child or people who are hurting or lonely, I want to go to them and help them, because I know that God wants to reach out to them. Much of the world today is looking out the window, with their noses pressed to the glass, and they're wondering if anyone is noticing, if anyone sees their need or their pain. If we would allow the truth of God to penetrate our minds, receive the love of God in our hearts, and then *release* God's truth and love into the world—like a river of life, like the channel of blessing it is intended to be—everyone in the world who is hurting, lonely, or in despair would find peace and hope and rest.

> God sees what is in our hearts. He loves us like a father. He cares about what we care about.

God sees what is in our hearts. He loves us like a father. He cares about what we care about. Even when we seem not to care about Him, He always cares about us, and He's always watching over us—even before we come to trust Him with our lives and realize that every good and perfect gift comes from above.

"Don't You Want to Go to Jesus?"

During my years in Austin, I didn't have much money or many material things, but I made the best of what I had. I used to look forward to Christmas presents and birthday presents from my aunt and my foster parents. But starting when I turned nine, and all the way up until I was fourteen, I didn't hear from my aunt or the Hales at all. That was very traumatic for me—and, if not for the grace of God, it might have destroyed me—because I thought that the people who had said they loved me had forgotten me.

One October, when my birthday came and I didn't get gifts from anybody, I remember thinking, *Anybody can forget a birthday, but they won't forget me at Christmas.*

That December, I painted a watercolor picture on a sheet of paper and hung it on the wall, and that was our Christmas tree and our decorations, because we couldn't afford to buy a tree or ornaments. When Christmas arrived and nothing came from my aunt or the Hales, I remember thinking, *They said they loved me, but they don't.*

That put a really big hole in my heart, made me feel as if I couldn't trust anyone, and caused me to doubt people's word. Even after I got into ministry, only the grace of God was able to lift me beyond the trauma of feeling forgotten.

When I was about fourteen, during a time when my mother was having some sort of trouble, she told me I could call the Hales and go stay with them for a week or so. I was afraid to call them, because I didn't know if they'd want me. But they sounded happy to hear from me and said they would come get me the very next day.

During that visit with the Hales, I had a lot of fun with the kids at their church. On Sunday night, which was right before the Monday or Tuesday when I would be going home, Pastor Hale asked the young people in the church to share what Jesus meant to them. Five or six kids stood up and gave testimonies that were really moving.

Then Pastor Hale gave the invitation, and when he said, "Would you come and put your hand in my hand, indicating that you want to give your life to the same Jesus that these kids have talked about?" all I could do was grip the chair in front of me. I was so shy, and so terrified, that I just hung on.

Then I saw Mrs. Hale walking toward me, with tears flowing so freely down her face that she had to hold her glasses in place with one hand. She put her other hand on my shoulder and said, "James, don't you want to go to Jesus?"

I said, "Yes, ma'am, but I'm afraid."

"I'll go with you," she said. "Could we go together?"

"Yes, ma'am."

I stepped out into the aisle and went forward with her, and in the best way I knew how, I trusted Jesus. As I've said many times since that night, I put my hand in the *pastor's* hand, but I put my life in the *Master's* hand.

I found out years later that, during the week I was visiting, Mrs. Hale had gone to all the Training Union groups—which were discipleship classes focused on missions and Baptist doctrine—and she had told them, "We have James with us, the boy who lived with us when he was a young child up until he was five, and now he's fourteen, and he's going back to his mother's place in the next day or two. Would you pray that tonight he'll give his life to Christ?" And sure enough, I gave my life to Christ that night.

This being a Baptist church, they took me right up and baptized me that night—right in my clothes because they didn't have a robe. A few years later, when I first started preaching and gave that testimony, somebody asked me, "If they baptized you in your clothes, what did you do when you came out of the water? If your clothes were all wet, what did you wear?"

The question caught me off guard, because I couldn't remember. The next time I saw Mrs. Hale, I asked her, "Didn't y'all take me right back and baptize me after I trusted Christ?" When she said yes, I asked, "Well, what did I do about clothes?"

Mrs. Hale started crying and said, "James, before I ever left for church that night, I took a change of clothes for you and put them back by the baptistery. That way, if you got saved, we'd have clothes for you."

That's how much faith, hope, and confidence my foster mother had. In later years, when I was preaching my crusades, Mrs. Hale would come to me after a service where hundreds of people had come to Christ, and she would say, "You know, son, when I watched all those people coming forward, I remembered the night I came and put my hand on your shoulder, and I'm so glad I did." Here was one lady who touched the life of a boy, and he went on to touch the lives of millions. But it likely wouldn't have happened if not for her love and prayer and faith. So don't ever give up on your prayers. And don't ever give up on the people you're praying for. God may have a miracle in store.

All-Night Prayer Meeting

When I got back home to Austin and told my mother I had given my life to Christ, she would not accept it. "I'll know when God gets ready to save you," she said. "You don't tell me."

"Well, Mother, I gave my life to Jesus."

Though my mother wouldn't accept my decision, I told a friend of mine whose dad was also an alcoholic and was never around, and he decided to accept Jesus too. We were out in the woods one night, a full moon in the sky, and I looked up and said, "My Father made that moon."

"Mine did too," my friend said, "because now we have the same Father."

"We sure do."

That was on a Thursday night, and the two of us stayed out in the woods and prayed all night long. Years later, in all six hundred or so of my citywide crusades, Thursday night was, by far, the night when I received the most responses. I would normally have a special youth emphasis on Thursdays, and I would preach a message about the difference between sex and love. The biggest crowds and the largest number of professions of faith were almost always on Thursday night. I can't help but believe that maybe those two teenage boys who prayed all night long on a Thursday were sowing seeds that bore eternal results.

Joe Robison

During that next year, my sophomore year in high school, my biological father came back into my life. My mother and I were staying with a different aunt this time, in a house that actually fronted onto a street. One day a man drove up out front and parked his car halfway onto the curb in the yard. My mother called me to the door and said, "Come here, son. Joe Robison's here. He's your daddy."

A tall man, about six feet two, got out of the car and started staggering toward the house. He came inside, smelling of booze, and we visited for a while, and I can remember thinking, with the hopeful naïveté of a boy who had grown up without a dad, *Maybe he can play catch with me sometime.*

I soon found out he couldn't throw a ball to save his life. I tossed him a football one time, and he grabbed it by the point and threw it back end-over-end like a helicopter propeller. I suppose it was no surprise. All he had ever done since he was nineteen years old was open whiskey bottles and beer cans.

When my mother got another in-home nursing assignment, and we moved into the patient's house, my father came to live with us as well. I didn't understand why my mother would allow a man who had raped her back into her life, but I had no say in the matter.

I had purchased a motor scooter with money from my job, so I now had transportation and didn't have to walk as much. I was really careful out on the roads, but one day a police car turned right in front of me, and I had a terrible wreck.

Just before the collision, the police officer saw me and instantly accelerated, and his car lurched forward so that I almost missed him altogether. If he had braked instead, I would have hit the car broadside and would have certainly been killed.

With no time to react, all I could do was hit the brakes, lay my bike down, and hope for the best. Like most people in those days, I wasn't wearing a helmet. They weren't required and were seldom worn by anyone. But though I miraculously avoided cracking my head open, I took off the back part of the police car—the bumper and taillights—with my right thigh. To this day, my leg has a big indentation where the muscles were compressed in toward the bone.

After radioing for an ambulance, which came pretty quickly, the officer came over, picked me up, and moved me onto the grass median. He was really shaken.

"I'm so sorry, son," he said more than once.

He followed the ambulance to the hospital and later visited me in the hospital and at home and became a real friend.

I got an insurance settlement from the scooter wreck, but I didn't want to buy another scooter, so I bought a .30-06 rifle, pre-64 Winchester model 70, hoping that one day I'd be able to go hunting with it.

One day my dad came home in a drunken rage and choked my mother until she passed out. Thinking he had killed her, he left the house and drove off.

When I came home from school that day, my mother had marks on her neck. When she told me what had happened, I became really angry.

"Son," she said, "if I hadn't passed out, he would have killed me."

I don't remember if it was later that day or sometime the next day, but my father came in drunk again, and when he found out my mother wasn't home, he started cursing me and threatened to kill me.

When he sat down in a chair, still cursing me, I ran back toward my bedroom, where I had a baseball bat leaning up against the wall just inside the door. I grabbed the bat and looked back to see if my dad was coming after me. If he'd been there, I would have hit him. That's how scared I was.

When I saw that he hadn't followed me, I dove under my bed and grabbed my rifle. This was just a few days after I had shot an oil can filled with water and blew a hole in it the size of a softball, so I knew what it could do.

I chambered a bullet, went back to the front room, and sat down on a little stool by the telephone, which was mounted on the wall. Sitting maybe twenty feet away from my father, and with the safety off, I pointed the rifle at him and said with all the firmness I could muster, "If you move so much as a finger, I'm gonna blow a hole in you big enough for someone to crawl through."

I reached for the phone, dialed 0, and asked the operator to send the police. "My father threatened to kill me," I said, "but I'm going to shoot *him*."

Within ten minutes, the sheriff's deputy who had hit me with his car was standing at the front door. He had been to the house many times after the accident to visit me, so the minute he heard the address on the emergency call, he came right over.

Here's the living amazed part: although my father sat there cursing me and calling me every name under the sun, he never moved a finger. If he would have so much as raised his hand to scratch his cheek, I would have shot him. And I would not have missed. At age fourteen, my world would have been turned upside down. Who knows what would have happened. But I believe the prayers of Memorial Baptist Church of Pasadena, and the people who had been praying for years for the little boy who had stayed with the Hales, froze my father and kept me from killing him.

> Don't ever give up on your prayers, and don't ever give up on the people you're praying for.

That story is part of the miracle of my life, and that's why I tell people, "Don't ever give up on your prayers, and don't ever give up on the people you're praying for." We don't always see our prayers answered, or answered in the way we would choose, but prayer is like love—it doesn't fail. And it's an amazing privilege to be able to pray for people.

Living with the Hales

My dad ended up in the penitentiary for seven or eight years. But even though he was out of the picture and my mother and I didn't have to worry about him anymore, I knew I couldn't stay in Austin. So I asked my mother if I could visit the Hales for the summer.

I spent the entire summer in Pasadena, and that's when I met Betty. When I first saw her at vacation Bible school, I thought she was the cutest little thing. And on Sunday nights in Training Union, when she was up front and she would turn around and smile at me, she wiped me out. It wasn't long before I was head over heels.

I asked her one time if she would leave Texas and go with me to Alaska to look for gold. She said, "I'll go." We were just kids, but she meant it, and I meant it. Instead, God turned our lives inside out, and together we've been seeking God, not gold, ever since.

By the end of the summer, Betty and I were so in love that I knew I had to stay in Pasadena. I went back to Austin and told my mother I was going to move in with the Hales. I told her that Brother Hale was coming to get me, and he was bringing Betty. I really wanted my mother to meet Betty.

But she was inconsolable, and she cried all evening.

A year or two later, in conversation with the Hales, I asked them why I had stopped hearing from them after my ninth birthday. They told me that they had sent presents for me every year—for my birthday, Christmas, and special occasions—but my mother had sent them all back. And she had sent back the presents from my aunt, as well. Well, that really shocked and hurt me. The next time I saw my mother, I asked her why she had done that.

"Well, I could never give you anything," she said, "and when you got all those presents, and I could see your excitement, I just really wanted you to love *me*."

Here was a woman whose parents had died when she was young—one when she was nine and the other when she was eleven—and she had grown up without their love at an important time in her life. She had married very young and been divorced, and I think she just wanted to be loved. Everybody said she was beautiful, so she never had a problem with attracting men, but I don't know that she ever felt loved. Looking back, I realize that my mother just wanted her own little boy to love her with all his heart. And though it wasn't the best, and it hurt me, I understand now why she did what she did. But I knew none of that when I was fourteen years old.

When I got up the next morning and went into my mother's room, she was gone. The bed was unmade and there was a crumpled up piece of paper on the pillow. When I picked it up, it was a little bit moist, and the ink was smudged, but I could still read the note.

> Son, I'm sorry I couldn't wait to see your girlfriend. I sure wanted to meet her. But I cried all night, and I didn't want her to see me the way I looked. I love you, son. I wish you weren't going.

When I read that, I just crumbled.

A friend of mine, Larry Wilson, had ridden the bus with me to Austin to help me gather my few belongings, and if he hadn't been there with me, I don't think I would have left Austin. He came into the room and said, "James, come on, man. Betty's coming to get you. We're going to play football, and we're going to play basketball and baseball, and you're going to get to do all the stuff that you never got to do. Come on, man. We're gonna have fun!" Without Larry's encouragement and friendship, I doubt I would have left. God used him in my life at a critical time.

When Brother Hale and Betty arrived, I put my stuff in the car and we drove back to Pasadena. When the school year started, I played three sports and did well in all of them. It was as easy for me as breathing. By the time I graduated, I had a scholarship offer to play basketball at San Jacinto Junior College, but I didn't take it—and they went on and won the national championship without me. But God didn't want my life to be wrapped up in sports, and it's obvious that He was protecting me. I said no to some things that seemed important, because God was calling me to do the most important thing for my life.

What the Bible Says about
LIVING AMAZED

The Father loves the Son and shows him all he does. Yes, and he will show him even greater works than these, so that you will be amazed.

John 5:20 NIV

The Jews there were amazed and asked, "How did this man get such learning without having been taught?"

John 7:15 NIV

An angel appeared to Moses in the flames of a burning bush in the desert near Mount Sinai. When he saw this, he was amazed at the sight.

Acts 7:30–31 NIV

3

Answering the Call

[The demon-possessed man] went away and began
to proclaim in Decapolis what great things Jesus had
done for him; and everyone was amazed.

Mark 5:20

As WE BEGAN our senior year of high school, Betty wanted me to
become more involved at church. But I was never excited about
religious life—and I'm still not. I'm excited about people who
are in love with Jesus, but a lot of what goes on in the church,
practicing the traditions of men rather than learning and applying
the Word of God, I can do without. The apostle Paul refers to
"worldly and empty chatter" that "will lead to further ungodli-
ness."[1] He also tells us to "refuse foolish, ignorant speculations,
knowing that they produce quarrels."[2] Even as a teenager, I had
already seen enough of that.

When the youth were planning a series of revival services the
next summer after I graduated, Betty kind of manipulated the
group to elect me as youth pastor so I would have to be there

every night. Part of my duties included welcoming the visiting evangelist and presiding on the platform during the services.

I'll never forget the night when sixteen-year-old Daniel Vestal came to lead that youth revival at our church. His command of Scripture was amazing—especially for such a young man. He had entire books of the Bible memorized, and he drew on this storehouse of wisdom to vigorously preach the gospel.

Being an athlete, I had a bit of a competitive spirit, and I remember thinking, *If he can do it, I can do it.* So during the rest of that eight-day revival, Betty and I began reading the Bible together, and I started trying to memorize a lot of Scripture. I found I had a good memory, and we were having a lot of fun with the fact that I could memorize so many passages. But I also began to see that the verses I memorized were affecting the way I lived my life. Over the past fifty-five years, it has been amazing to see how many of those Scriptures became significant in my life and ministry, including these:

- I beseech you therefore, brethren, by the mercies of God, that ye present your bodies a living sacrifice, holy, acceptable unto God, which is your reasonable service. And be not conformed to this world: but be ye transformed by the renewing of your mind, that ye may prove what is that good, and acceptable, and perfect, will of God.[3]
- Let this mind be in you, which was also in Christ Jesus: Who, being in the form of God, thought it not robbery to be equal with God: But made himself of no reputation, and took upon him the form of a servant, and was made in the likeness of men: And being found in fashion as a man, he humbled himself, and became obedient unto death, even the death of the cross. Wherefore God also hath highly exalted him, and given him a name which is above every name: That at the name of Jesus every knee

should bow, of things in heaven, and things in earth, and things under the earth; and that every tongue should confess that Jesus Christ is Lord, to the glory of God the Father.[4]

- And I, brethren, when I came to you, came not with excellency of speech or of wisdom, declaring unto you the testimony of God. For I determined not to know any thing among you, save Jesus Christ, and him crucified. And I was with you in weakness, and in fear, and in much trembling. And my speech and my preaching was not with enticing words of man's wisdom, but in demonstration of the Spirit and of power: That your faith should not stand in the wisdom of men, but in the power of God.[5]

- And ye shall be brought before governors and kings for my sake, for a testimony against them and the Gentiles. But when they deliver you up, take no thought how or what ye shall speak: for it shall be given you in that same hour what ye shall speak. For it is not ye that speak, but the Spirit of your Father which speaketh in you.[6]

On Friday night of the revival, I was up on the platform in support of Daniel Vestal, and I heard the Lord say to me very clearly, "I'm going to use you to preach My truth to the world."

I've often said that when the Lord speaks to me, I hear Him *louder* than if He were speaking out loud. This was the first time I had ever heard Him speak to me like this, but His word to me was loud and clear: "I want you to be an evangelist."

This was a mind-blowing prospect for an illegitimate child whose father had deserted him before he was ever born; whose mother had given him away by placing an ad in the newspaper; who had grown up feeling overlooked, unloved, totally rejected, and almost invisible. And now God was saying to me, "Son, *I see* you. *I choose* you. And I want to use you."

38

"God, how?" I asked. "How would I ever make a living as an evangelist?"

"Where is your faith?" the Lord replied.

I said, "It's all in You." And I meant it. I yielded my life into the Master Potter's hand; I gave Him the whole lump of clay.

As I sat there on the platform, it truly was a Holy Spirit–infilling moment. It was as if the Spirit of God swept me up and began to carry me along. He began to shape something in me—I wouldn't call it self-confidence but God-confidence—and the kind of boldness revealed in the book of Acts. I felt the power of that boldness and a legitimate compassion for others that just seemed to communicate and resonate with people. And it started instantly.

Charles Finney described his first encounter with the Holy Spirit as "waves of liquid love" flowing into his being. Like Finney, I could not express it any other way. I was immersed, enveloped, and overcome by an overwhelming sensation of love. I felt accepted, empowered, and inspired all at once. I was saturated with boldness; I was saturated with a confidence that I *still* long to see in every believer. Many people today walk in a spirit of intimidation and fear. Because the apostles had been with Jesus, the New Testament church was characterized by confidence. They had boldness. And out of their innermost being flowed rivers of life.

> The New Testament church was characterized by confidence. They had boldness. And out of their innermost being flowed rivers of life.

During the invitation, I told Pastor Hale that God was calling me to be an evangelist, and he announced it to the church. Afterward, people came up to me and shook my hand, but I don't know if they actually believed I could preach. Because I was so shy, I think some people thought God had been calling somebody else and I just happened to overhear it.

After the service, one of the deacons walked up to me and said, "Hey, James, how are you doing?"

"Do you think God can use me?" I asked.

"No," he said, and he walked away.

It was as if he was saying, *There's no way, James. You're too shy. You cannot be used.*

How's that for an encouraging start?

Preaching at Petro-Tex

On the following Monday, I went back to my summer job at the Petro-Tex chemical plant in Pasadena. I had been working as a painter's helper in town, but when a job opened up at Petro-Tex, I moved over there because I could make a little more money. I worked as a pipe fitter's assistant on a construction site, helping the men who were assembling all the pipes for a big addition to the plant. This was during the summer after I graduated from high school, right before I went off to East Texas Baptist College, and I had been working there for about three weeks when God called me to preach.

The plant workers ate lunch out in the yard every day, where there were several large flatbed trucks parked. As many as a hundred men would gather, put their lunch pails up on the flatbed trucks, and eat their sandwiches. To a shy kid, it was a big crowd.

The conversations during these lunchtimes were typically obscene and degrading. On top of all the cursing, the primary things these men talked about were all the bars and parties they were going to, all the women they were having sex with, and whatever else they were doing on the weekends. It was just awful, nothing but filth.

So there I was, having just received the call to preach, and I was surrounded by some of the vilest and most depraved talk you could ever hear—and it made me sick. I couldn't eat my lunch. As I looked around at all these men laughing and talking about how "we went to this party . . . and everyone was getting drunk and carrying on . . . ," I suddenly felt compelled to jump up onto one of the flatbed trucks and shout with the authority of a coach or a drill sergeant, "Listen! Listen to me!"

The men all turned and stared in my direction.

"Listen!" I said. "I'm just a boy trying to learn how to be a man, and all I'm hearing from you all is how to think filthy, talk filthy, and live filthy. Men, I wouldn't talk about a *dog* the way most of you talk about your wives."

The minute I said that, hot tears started cutting a course down my cheeks, which were covered in dust from the morning's work. I reached into the back pocket of my Levi's, where I had a little Soul Winner's New Testament. I held it up, with those tears in my eyes, and said, "But God loves you so much. He gave Jesus to die for you and to give you life, to show you how to live and how to love your wife and your family. I just want you to know that if I can help you, I'm a helper. If you will just call me, I will tell you how you can know Jesus."

> God loves you so much. He gave Jesus to die for you and to give you life.

With that, I jumped down off the truck. Without question, within me was a zeal and a fire that can only be described as the work of the Holy Spirit. I knew I had been caught up in a powerful force unlike anything I had ever experienced.

Now, with that many hardened souls standing around, you can imagine the kind of feedback I might have received. But there was none of that—no catcalls, no shouting, and no mockery. Only dead silence and a yard full of men, their mouths crammed with entire halves of sandwiches, staring at me in disbelief.

For the next three weeks, before I left for college, I led men to Christ all over that plant. I mean, it was nonstop, every day, praying with those men. I don't recall doing one lick of pipe fitting work. Instead, all day long, I would hear shouts of, "Helper! Helper!" and I would climb up onto the steel catwalks of the storage tanks they were working on, and the men would say, "You hit me, son. That's me. You were right. I don't love my wife like I should. I don't treat my kids like I should." And I would pray with them. I was seventeen years old, and I was catching my first glimpse of what it means to live amazed.

Years later, when we held crusades in the greater Houston area, men would come up to me after I had preached and say, "Five years ago . . . eight years ago . . . ten years ago, you led me to the Lord out there at the chemical company. We were way up on a catwalk and we got down on our knees." I met four who had become deacons in their church.

That's the way my ministry started. And the amazing results never stopped.

"You Go Preach"

I left Pasadena in September 1961, during the run-up to Hurricane Carla, one of the biggest storms ever to hit the Gulf Coast. The winds were blowing more than one hundred miles per hour as I drove my little Nash Rambler northeast toward Marshall, home of East Texas Baptist College (now East Texas Baptist University). As I drove in the right-hand lane, gusts of wind would blow my car sideways into the left-hand lane. This happened several times before I got far enough inland on Highway 59 to escape the worst of the storm. But the winds were that powerful.

I arrived in Marshall and moved into my room in Feagin Hall. I was rooming with Betty's brother, Pete, and it was nice to have at least one familiar face around campus, as I was still pretty shy with the other students.

I've always been curious and asked a lot of questions. I figured if I could find out what everyone else knew, and add it to what I already knew, then I'd be a little bit ahead of everyone. So I asked questions about whatever came to mind.

One night a bunch of us were hanging out in the dorm, and I asked a question that the other kids thought was dumb—something a little freshman would ask, I suppose—and they started mocking me.

An upperclassman named Billy Foote was walking through the hall and heard the kids laughing at me. I had kind of moved off to the side to get out of the line of fire, and Billy came over to me and said, "Hey, I want to tell you something. I see something in you that I don't see in all these guys who are making fun of you."

The minute he said that, it was like hearing the voice of the father I had never known. And coming from Billy, who was the most popular kid in school, it really meant a lot. He was one of those guys who was always telling jokes, and the other students went crazy when he entertained at the school talent show. He used to say, "I'm so popular that I've been president of the freshman class four years in a row."

I thanked him for what he said, and then I added, "I know you're really busy, Billy, but would you ever want to come by some night and pray with me?"

He said, "I sure will. Matter of fact, I'll come pray with you every night. What's your room number?"

And thus began one of most enjoyable and fruitful friendships of my life. I can remember lying in bed at night, looking at the crack under the door, waiting for Billy Foote to show up. He was always late. But I would wait patiently until I saw his feet at the base of the door. Then I would jump out of bed, and he and I would go down to the prayer room and pray together.

After we'd been doing this for several weeks, I said, "You know, Billy, I go out to the woods every day to pray, and I want to tell you something, if you promise you won't laugh at me."

"I promise," he said. "I won't laugh."

"I was out there the other day, just sitting on a stump and talking to Jesus. And He told me that, in a real short time, I'm going to be preaching in some of the biggest churches in the country. And in a matter of years, I'm going to be preaching in stadiums. And I've never even preached. Not once. Do you think I'm crazy?"

Billy was sitting across the room from me—it was just a small prayer room—and he got up and walked over and dropped down on his knees in front of me. He put his hand on my knee, looked me in the eye, and said, "I don't think you're crazy. But you know what I want you to do?"

"What?"

"I want you to get down on your knees with me right now, and I want us to pray together that when God does what He wants to do with you, you won't ever get in His way."

And that's what we prayed.

Then Billy said, "You know, I'm the director of the Baptist Student Union choir, and we go out to churches. It's one of the ways that the school recruits students. I want you to go with us next time. You can give a little testimony and then introduce the choir."

So I started going with him—but it didn't last long, because I messed everything up from the get-go. I'd get up to introduce the choir, and I might speak for five minutes, but there were times when the choir wouldn't get to sing because people all over the building would be weeping and coming down the aisles to accept the Lord and get right with God.

It was literally that amazing.

The choir just stood there in disbelief—and so did I—because it made no sense that a shy young man with no experience could stand up and share his heart for just a few minutes and get that kind of response.

After a few nights like that, Billy came to me and said, "James, I've led a lot of revivals, but nothing like this. Why don't we go see some preachers in the area and tell them we're going to be an evangelistic team. I'll do the music and you preach. Let's go see if we can get some revivals."

Well, it excited me that the most popular kid in school wanted to team up with me. But when we went out and talked to the churches, half of the preachers laughed at us. One of the pastors who didn't know quite what to think of us was Jimmy Draper, who later became my pastor in the Dallas-Fort Worth area. Jimmy asked us if we had some recommendations.

I said, "No, sir, we don't have any recommendations, because I haven't preached yet. But we believe God wants us to do this."

"Well," he said, "let's wait a little while and see what happens."

Years later, I was a member of a church that called Jimmy Draper as pastor, and about eight hundred people in the congregation were affiliated in some way with my ministry. I was able to tell the church, "We've got a pastor here who was one of the first ones to tell me no when I asked if I could preach." Jimmy and I had a good laugh about that.

Though Billy Foote was a key person God used to help me get started, Billy was my singer for only a year. He wasn't a soloist, and we felt we needed a soloist for the way most revivals and crusades were conducted in those days. Then I met John McKay, and though I'd been preaching for only a year at that point, John agreed to become my soloist—forming a partnership that would last for decades. Billy understood and was happy to hand me off.

Even though some pastors were hesitant at first to have Billy and me come in to do a revival, their reluctance didn't last long. I would speak at one church and twenty-five other churches would call to try to book me. And this was all by word of mouth. We weren't sending out mailings or anything—it was a total spiritual explosion.

R. G. Lee, who was known as the prince of preachers, took me under his wing and introduced me to all sorts of different settings. He said, "James, I've never seen anything like it. I'm supposed to be a gifted communicator, but I couldn't even begin to do what you do. I take you into a typing class, a women's club, a civic club, a school, an auditorium, or a church building, and the whole place is electrified, moved, and captivated." I agreed that it was remarkable, and I was as amazed as anyone.

During the week of each revival, I would speak at the local high schools, and at the end of my message I would say, "Some of you here today may laugh at me. You may mock me. But as you go home today, I want you to remember that a man came to your school—and nobody paid him a nickel to come—and he came because he cared about you and wanted to share how a friend had changed his life. I will talk about that friend tonight at the meeting where I'm speaking. I invite you all to come." And then I'd go on my way.

If the administrators wouldn't let me speak at a school, I would just walk the hallways. (I couldn't do that today; I'd be arrested.) I didn't talk to anybody; I was just there. By lunchtime, everybody would be talking about the man in the hallway. And it wasn't long before they figured out I was the guy doing the crusade in the nearby stadium, coliseum, or church. And some of them would show up that night to hear me preach.

Before long, I was preaching in so many places and going so many different directions that I missed the maximum number of classes I could miss at East Texas Baptist and still pass. I met with the president of the college, Dr. Howard Bennett, and told him what was happening.

"I've got all these crusades in all these big churches," I said. "What do you want me to do?"

"Whatever you do, James, we're going to cover you here at school. You go preach."

So, with Dr. Bennett's blessing, I went to preach an eight-day revival at First Baptist Denton. The building was overflowing with people every night, and it was glorious—and I was missing every class back at school.

By Wednesday night of that week, I was so sick and burning up with fever that we called a doctor to my room. He came and examined me and said, "Man, you have got a serious case of the chicken pox."

"Oh, I feel terrible," I said. "But I'm preaching a revival at First Baptist, and the place is packed every night. Is this stuff contagious?"

"*Contagious?*" the doctor said. "All you have to do is be in the same room with them and they've got it."

"Well, what am I going to do with this great revival and all these people coming from all over town?"

"You go up there and preach, chicken pox and all," the doctor said. "If they haven't had 'em, they need 'em."

So I preached the rest of the week with chicken pox broken out all over me, and people kept coming forward to get saved. When I told the people what I had, they kept coming anyway. I suppose that's an example of the gospel "going viral." Though it's hard to imagine something like that happening today in our risk-averse times, it shows how the power of God's Word grabbed ahold of people whenever I would preach.

The revivals during those early years were so staggering that, when I look back on it now, it defies imagination. Add to that the various endorsements I began to receive from some of the most renowned preachers in America, and it was positively mind-blowing.

Here's what W. A. Criswell, longtime pastor of First Baptist Church in Dallas, wrote in a letter to his fellow pastors in the Southern Baptist Convention:

> Once in a generation, a star arises on the spiritual horizon whose beams fall upon uncounted thousands in pristine glory and celestial power. One such star is James Robison. He is an evangelist called of God, and his voice is like that of John the Baptist, urging the people to repentance and to faith in Jesus, our Lord.
>
> He is a God-made preacher. The Lord in heaven bestowed upon him ten talents. All ten he has dedicated fully and completely in the service of the Master. In answer to his appeal, the Holy Spirit bestows many souls. Whether in a church house or in a civic auditorium or in a football stadium, the power and presence of the Lord is upon him.
>
> With infinite gratitude to God for him and his ministry, we are looking forward to the years that lie ahead in which he will be increasingly used by the Holy Spirit to preach the gospel of Christ. No young man has had a greater or more effectual door opened before him than James Robison. God bless him in the great work, and God use him to win untold multitudes to the Savior.[7]

And then there was this from O. C. Robinson of Shiloh Terrace Baptist Church:

> My Brother Pastors:
>
> Permit me to introduce to you the greatest evangelistic team that has ever been in our church or that I have ever known during my 25 years in the ministry. We have just concluded the greatest revival meeting in the history of our church and the greatest outpouring of spiritual power I have ever witnessed in all my years in the work. In an eight-day meeting, we had 94 professions of faith, 21 additions by letter.
>
> The preaching of James Robison is the most powerful I have ever heard. Only a miracle of God could give to the world a boy of 19 with the wisdom, the knowledge and the spiritual power of

this young man. His preaching, his invitations, and his personal work are superior to most men who have years and years of experience and study. I believe he is heaven's gift for our day and time.

We recommend him to the pastors and churches of SBC without reservation.[8]

Endorsements like these led to my receiving a thousand invitations to preach in about six months—including twenty-eight from one city alone. That's what started our citywide crusades. We called all the pastors together and said, "We've got twenty-eight requests from churches in your town. Is there any chance y'all would go in together?"

Over the years, I've had many people ask me, "How does a person get started in evangelism?" How do I answer that question? What happened with me makes no sense. It certainly wasn't a pattern for others to follow. Nevertheless, if God could do amazing things with my life, and with the gifts He's given me, then He can do the same with you and your gifts. God can work with *anyone* who is yielded

> **God can work with anyone who is yielded to Him.**

to Him. Even if you're broken down, beaten up, or defeated, know that God is able to work all things together for good.[9] If we love God, everything will work for our good and God's glory, no matter how bad it looks. God knows what's best, and He knows His own plans.

Even though I had a boldness to preach right from the get-go, it doesn't mean I didn't get nervous. In fact, in the early years, my legs would shake so badly when I was sitting up on the platform waiting to preach that my knees would start bouncing up and down. The pastors would lay their hands across my knees and press my legs down to keep them from shaking. That's how bad it was. But the minute I stood up and took two steps toward the pulpit, I was enveloped with those liquid waves of God's Spirit—an immersion in boldness, fearlessness, and love—and the shaking went away.

That pattern persisted for about a year and a half, until one memorable night at Thomas Avenue Baptist Church in Pasadena. The building was overflowing, and we had already had about fifty young people and adults get saved on the first couple of nights of the revival. But as I walked up to the pulpit, the familiar feeling of immersion in boldness and power wasn't there.

I felt nothing.

I went into a state of panic, got distracted, and kind of stumbled my way through the message. And I probably gave a weak invitation.

When I got back to my room that night, the Lord had a crystal clear message for me: "I am *always* with you. Don't you *ever, ever* trust a feeling or a sensation—*ever again*. You. Trust. *Me*. Period."

He spoke to my spirit. I heard it and accepted it, and I never, ever feared again. And I never again looked for a feeling to validate the Lord's work in my life.

Meeting Billy Graham

It made no sense for a shy kid who grew up without a father to suddenly capture the attention of people everywhere—whether on a construction site, in a parking lot, on a school playground, or in a gymnasium. It didn't matter. And by the time I was nineteen years old, people were telling me that I would become the next Billy Graham.

Of course, I knew who Billy Graham was. By 1961, everybody did. So when God called me to become an evangelist, Billy was the first example that came to mind of what an evangelist was: someone who preached in extended meetings over several days. I had no idea that the meetings would quickly become citywide crusades or that I would go on to hold hundreds of them across the country over the next twenty-five years.

As me and my team began to gain some traction with our revivals, Billy Graham heard about how our meetings were being blessed and took the initiative to contact Fulbright & Jaworski, a Houston law firm that did a lot of work with nonprofits, and Paul Martin, a leading tax attorney and Baylor University board member, and together they established the proper groundwork for the James Robison Evangelistic Association and later helped us organize a board of directors. Billy had seen some others in ministry get hurt by their board members, and he wanted to make sure we got everything set up right. When he called to explain what he had done, he said plainly, "You're going to need this." That was such a tremendous gift and a great example of how Billy Graham has always supported and encouraged me.

Later on, when Billy's ministry activities brought him to Texas, we made a point of trying to get together for a visit, and we also occasionally talked on the phone.

When Billy's son, Franklin, began attending LeTourneau College (now LeTourneau University) in Longview, Texas, Billy asked me if I would reach out to Franklin, who at the time wasn't living for God. In his younger years, Franklin had faced exactly the opposite challenge that I had. Whereas I grew up without an earthly father to look to, Franklin grew up in the spotlight surrounding Billy Graham. Billy thought maybe I could help Franklin because we shared an interest in the outdoors and hunting and fishing. But though I did everything I could to get Franklin to meet with me, he just never would do it. Later, after he had become a Christian, I asked him what had happened during that time. He said, "I always just went out and smoked cigarettes and drank beer and stayed away from you."

It seemed to me that Billy had given me an assignment—that's basically what it was—to win his son to the Lord, but I was unsuccessful. Even though Franklin went through some pretty rough patches in his early years, it's a testimony to God's faithfulness—and yet another example of living amazed—that he came through, found his footing, and has since invested his life for God's purposes. LIFE Outreach has supported the work of Samaritan's Purse, which Franklin leads, and Betty and I have been to the Sudan with Franklin for a missions outreach. He and I are good friends to this day.

Billy and I continued to have discussions during the years of my evangelistic ministry. He asked me about various areas of the country where he hadn't been yet, about what the pastoral participation might be like, and what challenges I saw there. Through our discussions and prayer, we developed a wonderful friendship.

What the Bible Says about
LIVING AMAZED

Then a demon-possessed man who was blind and mute was brought to Jesus, and He healed him, so that the mute man spoke and saw. All the crowds were amazed.

Matthew 12:22–23

A crowd came together in bewilderment, because each one heard their own language being spoken. Utterly amazed, they asked: "Aren't all these who are speaking Galileans?"

Acts 2:6–7 NIV

Simon himself believed; and after being baptized, he continued on with Philip, and as he observed signs and great miracles taking place, he was constantly amazed.

Acts 8:13

4

Burnout

He could not do any miracles there, except lay his
hands on a few sick people and heal them. He was
amazed at their lack of faith.

Mark 6:5–6 NIV

THERE I WAS, fresh out of high school and with less than a year
of preaching experience, yet all I heard was, "You're the next
Billy Graham." I was told by several people that Billy himself
had come to believe that.

The people who told me those things were simply trying to
encourage me as a young evangelist, but the pressure actually
became more of a negative, like a weight on my shoulders, because I erroneously began to measure my life and my ministry
against Billy Graham's and what he did. It was as if we were in
some kind of contest to see whether I would surpass his successes. I never saw it as a competition—both Billy and I were
dedicated to winning souls for the kingdom of God, and Billy
was quite helpful and supportive to me along the way—but for

the next twenty-five years, that was the track I was on and those were the voices I heard.

According to Frank Harber, who wrote his PhD dissertation at Southwestern Baptist Theological Seminary on evangelism from the New Testament days to present time, I had spoken to more people face-to-face by the age of thirty than anyone else in history.[1] Of course, Billy Graham didn't have his first really big crusades until he was *in* his thirties, but the sheer number of times and places that I spoke and the fact that I preached to so many people at such a young age was truly miraculous.

But I was also exhausted.

Most evangelists at that time—and there were quite a number in the Southern Baptist Convention alone—held maybe five or ten crusades a year. I was doing anywhere from thirty-three to forty-one. And these were eight-day crusades, Sunday night to Sunday night. It was only far later in my ministry, when I was in my midthirties, that I might do a five-day or weekend-long crusade. But those were few and far between.

During the course of those eight-day crusades, I spoke at two or three high schools a day, at every civic club and every women's function in town, and I met with the city pastors at least three days at noon. On top of that, I met with all the young people from junior high through high school for a youth fellowship gathering at least every other night. At most crusades, it was *every* night, if the facility would accommodate it. And then of course I preached the main service. So I was speaking five to seven times a day, and I did this for 275 to more than 300 days a year, for two-and-a-half decades.

As I write this, the United States is in the middle of the 2016 presidential election process. When I compare my old crusade schedules with what these candidates are doing, from an energy, adrenaline, work, and travel perspective, I ran for president for nearly twenty-five years! That was the kind of schedule I kept all the time. I was consumed by the vision of winning the world to Christ, and everyone was saying, "God is using you. You've got to come to our city. We're in trouble, and you can help us." In Southern Baptist circles, where I got my start, they broke records for church growth and number of baptisms during those years. It was a high-impact time.

When I look back on it now, I can just about start to weep at how little time I was able to spend with my children when they were growing up. That they all love God the way they do is a miracle and a testimony to my wife, Betty, and the prayers of so many who heard me preach.

After spending more than twenty years living at this relentless pace, I was emotionally and spiritually drained, operating strictly in the gift of evangelism that God had placed on me but not living in the fruit of the Holy Spirit. I was irritable, impatient, angry, easily frustrated, and anything but Christlike in my spirit.

I no longer went to the Word of God to gain life, insight, and inspiration. I went to the Bible for one reason only: *to get sermons to preach to others.* The Bible had become a sermon book for me, rather than a book of life. And the more that became true, the more contentious and easily distracted I became.

I remember one day when I was first getting started, during the time I was attending East Texas Baptist, I was praying alone out in the woods and the Lord said to me, "You're going to be preaching before the largest churches, the largest stadiums all across the nation." He showed me a vision of stadiums and coliseums filled with people—and I hadn't even preached yet. I remember saying, "Well, it doesn't even matter, Lord. That's really nice and all, but it doesn't matter what happens or how big the crowds are. I'm always going to come back here to be with You. I'm going to be out here with You, talking to You and loving You." And it was as if the Lord said, "Really?" I remember it as if it just happened: *"Really?"* In other words, "Will you *really* come back here when all this happens?" And the fact is, I did *not* go back. I just got sermons and kept preaching. And people kept getting saved. And I was making myself vulnerable and sick.

The amazing thing is that God continued to bless His Word. He did not take His gifts away from me. Every good and perfect gift comes from the Father, but He's not one to renege on what He has given. His gifts can be misused and terribly abused, but if we're not yielded to and filled with His Spirit, the fruit of His Spirit will not be manifested.

I can assure you that the fruit of the Spirit was not at all evident in my life at that time. One of my longtime staff members said that meeting with me during those years was like meeting with a wounded bear. I tried to justify my anger as "righteous indignation," but it was carnal at every level. I was angry at everything that was out of place in the church or in anybody's life, including my own. The passion I displayed during those years was really just me shouting at my own tormentors, my own demons.

When people say they have to battle their own demons, they usually mean it figuratively. We Baptists in particular don't like to acknowledge that our spiritual problems have anything to do with actual demons. In fact, if you start talking about real demons, many people think you're not very intelligent, that you've moved back to the Dark Ages and are exercising a lack of intellectual rigor. I've heard it said that Jesus referred to demons only because He had to use language that ignorant people at the time would understand.

That's not true.

Jesus knew exactly what He was talking about. He understood better than anyone the forces of evil; the wicked, fiery darts of the devil; the realms of darkness and deception, principalities and powers. And the demons he cast out of people weren't *figurative*.

The spirit world is as real and alive as electricity, and the invisible realm is the most active realm in the universe. It's powerful.

In the unseen realm, we are constantly bombarded by signals and impulses. As someone once told me, "Not all the voices you hear are your own. Not all your *thoughts* are your own." The enemy's attacks often come to us as suggestions, ideas, and thoughts. We are barraged by this negative energy all the time, which is why we need to stay close to and follow the Word of God. Otherwise we can "walk in the way which is not good, following [our] own thoughts."[2]

> The spirit world is as real and alive as electricity, and the invisible realm is the most active realm in the universe.

In my spiritual upbringing in the church, we were taught to ignore all that. We'd talk about backsliding yet completely overlook the one who was greasing our wheels for destruction. But I was, without question, being tormented and defeated during this time in my life.

When I realized that something had gripped my mind, attitude, and spirit; that I didn't have love, joy, peace, and patience; that I wasn't gentle, kind, and meek, God brought me to my knees—literally. I was never accused of any wrongdoing, and I wasn't caught in any wrongdoing, but I was arrested by the convicting power of the Holy Spirit. The fact is, I had left my first love.[3] I had walked away from the vital, daily connection with Jesus I'd had when I was praying in the woods of East Texas. I missed the intimacy, the love, and the relationship with Him that I'd had when I started.

But God was about to get my attention.

In those days, a group of churches from a city or an area would contact our ministry to say they wanted to have an evangelistic outreach. T. D. Hall, our crusade director, would go in and meet with the pastors and begin to make the necessary arrangements. Sometimes, if it looked like a citywide crusade was going to be a big one, I would fly in, meet with the pastors, stir them up, and then leave it to them to get the process going. As the time for the crusade drew nearer, I would go back to the city and do a pre-crusade banquet to raise the majority of the budget. This was part of the schedule I ran that had me on the road more than three hundred days a year.

At one of those pre-crusade banquets, after I had told the organizing committee that I'd been in five states during the past three days, including two states that same day, a woman at the head table asked me, "When do you pray?"

I turned to her and said, "I don't! *You* pray! *I* preach!"

That's literally what I said to her, and she was visibly stunned.

I didn't know it at the time, but in that remark were the seeds of my deliverance, my eventual freedom. The sheer foolishness of my reply was part of what brought me under conviction. But that's what I actually thought: *I don't have* time *to pray. You all do the praying, and I'll preach.*

I knew the truth: Jesus didn't teach His disciples to *preach*. He taught them to *pray*. But me? I didn't need what His disciples needed, because I could handle the preaching. That's the arrogance of success, and that's what I had come to. Great success is a great test that most people don't pass. I certainly didn't. I failed. And I was paying the price.

> **Jesus didn't teach His disciples to preach. He taught them to pray.**

I knew something was missing. I knew I didn't love Jesus the way I once had. I was so disheartened that I didn't even want to continue in my ministry. I actually wished that I would go to sleep one night and never wake up. I felt that bad.

I remember Tom Elliff preaching at one of my Bible conferences, and he talked about how we get worn out and tired. He said, "I see these pastors, and it's like Samson grinding at the mill. He's lost his vision, and he's just grinding at the mill."[4]

I had gone to the upper reaches of the coliseum where our conference was being held and had curled up in one of the chairs, just trying to get away from it all for a few minutes. But when I heard what Tom said, I had to admit it: *That's me. That's what I feel like—Samson grinding at the mill.* But I was afraid that if I didn't keep preaching the Word, people would be lost, and it would be my fault.

Everything just wasn't right. I wasn't hearing God, and I remember crying out in desperation. At the same time, I was suffering from chronic sinus infections, and I had terrible sore throats. Somehow I always managed to keep my voice going, but my throat would be raw.

Nothing stopped me—I might have missed *one* night for illness out of the thousands of times I spoke—but I would go home hurting and feverish. I think I was eating terribly as well, and my stomach was all torn up. I knew I was a mess, and I knew I was desperate, but I didn't know what to do about it.

I kept asking Dudley Hall, my friend and longtime associate, "Can anyone really be free, to the point where we're not tormented?"

We were both so caught up in it that he couldn't even answer me.

"Do you know many people, Dudley, who are really free?"

He couldn't say yes, and neither could I.

Meanwhile, everywhere I went, in every city where I preached, I ended up counseling pastors and church leaders whose lives were a mess—many were caught up in affairs with women in their congregations. All those dealings broke my heart.

One night Dudley came to me and said, "I have a guy you need to meet. His name is Milton Green. He's a professional carpet cleaner, and he has only an eighth-grade education, but you need to meet him."

We invited Milt to come with us to our next speaking engagement, and that night 175 people accepted Christ when I gave the invitation. But when we went back to the hotel, Milt said to me, "James, I feel so sorry for you. I think you're one of the most tormented people I've ever met."

I knew it was true. I *was* tormented.

Milt asked if he could pray for me, and I said, "Okay."

We were sitting in my hotel room, just the two of us, and he began to pray simply and forcefully—but in an almost childlike way—taking authority over the tormenting spirits and combating the harassment I was under. He wasn't trying to promote a theology of deliverance or train me in a method of prayer. He was contending with almighty God for my life and freedom.

As an ambassador for Jesus Christ, Milt prayed powerfully for me, commanding every foul, lying, and tormenting spirit to get out of my life and get off God's property. He spoke with conviction, and I remember thinking, *I hope nobody hears him. This man's talking to the devil, and I'm the only one in the room.*

When he finished his prayer, he said, "How do you feel?"

"I don't feel anything," I said.

"You don't feel like something kinda lifted off of you, like a weight came off of you?"

"I don't feel anything."

"Well, it's over, son," Milt said, reaching over and slapping me on the leg. "The party line is going to get real quiet and you're going to start hearing God real clear."

Then he got up and walked out of my room.

I just shrugged.

I'm glad he's gone.

A few days after I got home from that trip, I woke up with tears literally rolling down my cheeks, and I was quoting Scripture verses out loud that I didn't know I had ever memorized. The words were flowing out of me like a river.

Betty was looking at me like I was a little bit crazy, but I said, "Honey, it's gone. It's gone."

"What's gone?" she said.

"That stinkin' claw that was in my brain. That grip has been broken."

And it was. In fact, the change was so remarkable that I can't adequately describe it, other than to say that calm had settled over the landscape of my soul and overwhelming peace filled my heart. Above all, the distractions and unhealthy attractions and other things that had contributed to my torment were gone. And a fruitfulness of the Spirit was so powerfully manifested that it captivated Betty.

> The change was so remarkable that I can't adequately describe it, other than to say that a calm had settled over the landscape of my soul and an overwhelming peace filled my heart.

Well, at first it alarmed her, because she thought, *Oh my goodness, what happened?* But the change was so obvious and so positive that soon she was rejoicing right along with me.

I said, "Honey, above everything else that God has done in my heart, He told me I'm supposed to preach to the *whole* church in the *whole* earth, to see the church get whole. And I will not be confined by any man-made wall or barrier. I'm going to take the gospel of Jesus Christ, and His love, to the ends of the earth—however God wants me to. And I'm going to speak to leaders and love them. That's what He showed me."

The Lord also made it clear that I'd be more effective sitting down than standing up. I initially misinterpreted what that meant and began to preach my crusades sitting on a stool or on the edge of the platform, because I thought maybe my style of delivery was distracting people and getting in God's way; that maybe people were just watching the dynamic preacher and weren't hearing what they needed to hear. So I became different in my demeanor. But that wasn't really what the Lord wanted me to understand.

Over time, He made two things clear about my sitting down. He said, "You will be sitting at My feet, listening to My words, and you will be sitting down with leaders, as a servant spokesman, talking to them. And you're going to be more effective as a servant, *sitting*, than you ever were when you preached the gospel to millions of people in all those coliseums, stadiums, and churches."

At the time, we had recorded two million professions of faith at our crusades. But in the years since, my staff has stopped trying to keep up with all the reports from all the outreaches our ministry supports worldwide—from film ministries in India to various crusades and ministries in North America and abroad. I've heard estimates as high as twenty million recorded commitments to Christ, but our efforts are not driven by the numbers. We're just supporting every effective outreach we can, and we'll continue to do that.

Too much pride is placed in numbers—and what does it all mean anyway? Only God knows the number of names that are written in the Book of Life. We just have to be faithful to the calling He has placed on our lives and leave the results to Him. The sheep know the Shepherd's voice, and He knows them.[5] We're not called to try to number the flock.

In fact, in 1 Chronicles it says that Satan is the one who moved King David to take a census in Israel.[6] When Joab, the king's faithful adviser, heard about it, he said, "May the Lord add to His people a hundred times as many as they are! But . . . are they not all my lord's servants? Why does my lord seek this thing?"[7] We can look at all the numbers, but what kind of real impact are we having on people's lives? That's what we should be concerned about.

As I have spent the latter half of my life sitting down—in a studio next to Betty, and with leaders all over the world, from Asia to Africa to all of North America—I have seen the impact of the Lord's work firsthand. Many of those stories will be told in the remaining pages of this book.

I chose to include the story of my midlife burnout, both as a cautionary example for those who are caught up in building their ministries but have walked away from their first love and for readers everywhere who may look at what Betty and I have done in our years of ministry and say, "Well, I could never do that, and therefore God can't use me in any meaningful way." That's simply not true. God is looking for *any* yielded heart, *any* member of the body of Christ who will be like clay in the hands of the Master Potter, any lump of clay that will allow God to form a holy vessel for His own purposes. Christ's body has no insignificant members. We all play a vital role.

I want to plant some seeds of hope in your heart, so that, as you read this book, you will know you're not merely reading about *someone else's* journey, you're reading about the very real possibility of what can happen to *you*, on *your* pilgrim journey, and the pilgrim's progress that *you* can make. I want you to know, without a doubt, that you can experience the hand of God on your life. Even amid the heat and pressure, God is making diamonds and refining gold for a radiant expression of His glory and countenance. We can live amazed by God's power, grace, and faithfulness, and we can be absolutely certain that even when we're knocked down, we don't stay down, because our loving Father is even more anxious to pick us up than we are to get up. And we can live in that reality. My prayer is that you will know it's true.

I began this account of living amazed with the story of my upbringing and the story of my rise and fall, because I've been on the bottom. I know what it's like to feel overlooked, overwhelmed, and forgotten. I've also received people's praise, and I believe we all want to feel loved, respected, and appreciated.

Through all my experiences, I have learned above all to desire our Father's approval. Many people have told me I'm a great encouragement to them, and I hope that's true, because I believe that building up the body of Christ is important. It means a great deal to have someone say, "You helped me, you blessed me, you pointed me to Jesus. Thank you." Yet all I want now is to hear the still, small voice of my heavenly Father saying to me, "Well done, James. I'm proud of you, son. You have been a good and faithful servant." I pray I will hear that when I stand before the Father in the eternal kingdom.

No matter what kind of life you're living right now, no matter what kind of life you've lived in the past, and no matter what kind of baggage you may carry—that past will not be your present. You will no longer allow the past to hold you prisoner. And you will not allow the *glory* of the past to cause you to live in the past. "For I am about to do something new. See, I have already begun! Do you not see it? I will make a pathway through the wilderness. I will create rivers in the dry wasteland."[8]

As you continue to move forward, you will be grateful for the memories, but you will press on to what lies ahead—the prize and the high calling of Christ Jesus to win the race that He has set before you.[9]

My prayer for you is that you will sense the Father's amazing presence and that you will know how special you are to Him. God loves you so much that He sacrificed His Son to save you. He longs to bless you and to bless others through you.

What the Bible Says about
LIVING AMAZED

At once the fig tree withered. Seeing this, the disciples were amazed.

Matthew 21:19–20

He did not answer him with regard to even a single charge, so the governor was quite amazed.

Matthew 27:14

His father and mother were amazed at the things which were being said about Him.

Luke 2:33

5

God's Amazing Unity

Everyone was amazed and gave praise to God. They were filled with awe and said, "We have seen remarkable things today."

Luke 5:26 NIV

BEFORE GOD USED the fervent prayer of a humble carpet cleaner to break through my burnout and stretch my faith through a marvelous, fresh encounter with the power of the Holy Spirit and a real outpouring of God's love, freedom, and fullness in my life, I was a hard-line, fundamentalist, right-wing Baptist—very conservative and very outspoken. Some would have even called me extreme. Jerry Falwell told me I made other conservative preachers look like liberals, if that gives you any idea.

Like many conservative evangelicals, I felt it was my duty to hold the line against other groups that didn't line up with my understanding of Scripture.

Billy Graham and I are both Southern Baptists, and as a Baptist I couldn't understand why he was working with so many

Catholics, Pentecostals, and charismatics in his ministry. I called Billy one time, and during our conversation I scolded him for having all those kinds of people on the platform with him at his crusades. I told him I didn't understand it, and I wondered if maybe he was compromising.

I didn't know it at the time, and it didn't happen right away, but Billy's response would change the course of my life. Over time it became one of the most life-changing conversations I've ever had and completely transformed my ministry.

When I told Billy my concerns about what he was doing, he asked me, "Do you know these people that you're telling me to stay away from?"

"No, I don't know them."

"Well, I do," he said. "And I'd like to suggest that you spend time with some people you've been taught to avoid."

That may not be good advice to a child, but for an adult—for people in the church and certainly for church leaders—it was one of the greatest bits of advice I've ever received.

When Billy and I had that conversation, I was still keeping a full schedule of crusades and working toward my eventual burnout. I was still pretty tough, and strongly principled, but I was also intolerant of anyone who disagreed with what I understood as truth. I came across as bitterly angry. One reason why we should love our enemies is that they will tell us the truth that often others won't tell us. But even the fact that I would view people who disagreed with me as *enemies* tells you something about my state of mind at the time.

> **One reason why we should love our enemies is that they will tell us the truth that often others won't tell us.**

Compassion Breaks Down Walls

After the Lord did His deep work in my life, I realized I had been operating out of an unhealthy rage—and God delivered me from it. I didn't lose my convictions or the value of my principles, but as I began spending time with people outside my Baptist circles, I came to understand in a whole new way that truth must be spoken in love and that love never fails. I saw how compassion breaks down walls and opens hearts and minds. My entire life was changed in so many ways by what Billy Graham said to me that day on the phone.

I began to meet with people I'd been taught to avoid. I went to visit Oral Roberts and asked if I could just talk with him. We sat in a little room in the Mabee Center at Oral Roberts University, just the two of us, and I confessed that I had been critical of him, that I had been unkind, that I had made fun of him, and I realized I was wrong. And I asked Oral to forgive me for the way I had treated him in the past.

I could now see that he had been cut off from other parts of the Christian community because he did things that others didn't understand—for example, he emphasized healing prayer.

I told him, "God has shown me that the only reason you ever had the healing lines is because Christians don't pray for one another like we should. We give lip service to the power of God, but we don't have an active faith that believes He is the same yesterday, today, and forever; that He can still do the same miracles He did in the New Testament; and that He can still heal. We ought to be doing what the Bible says—laying hands on the sick and praying for them—and it shouldn't be left up to Oral Roberts, or anyone else, to have lines of people coming for healing prayer. We should be ministering to the needs of people in our local congregations."

"Oh, I've longed for that," he said. "There never should have been a healing line. We never should have needed one. The whole church needs to pray for their own family members, their own church members. And we just need to reach out in love to one another. That's what God wants."

"I've been so lonely in this ministry," he continued. "I feel as if I've been an island unto myself. And there have been times when I would pray for hours and hours for all these people, and sometimes I would have to hand a little crippled child back to the mother and watch the mother either carry the child away or wheel the child off in a wheelchair, and I would say to them, 'I'm so sorry.' And they would turn back and say, 'It's okay, Oral. At least you tried.'"

When he said that, it really touched my heart, and I thought, *Why do we as Christians make fun of one another instead of working together and trying to learn from one another? We should be praying for all these sick people and asking God for a miracle.*

We all know that sometimes physical healing doesn't happen, and we have to ask God instead for the miracle of healing our broken hearts. I can't ever talk about answered prayer without thinking about the prayers we prayed for our beautiful daughter Robin, who died of cancer at the age of forty. She never once wavered in her faith, and neither did we. And yet she died. Sometimes we have to pray for the grace of God to help us walk through the pain of not getting our desired miracle and not understanding why. Betty and I learned that lesson firsthand. Prayer may not operate on our time frame or our schedule, and it may not be up to our expectations, but it's still a miracle in action. So we must pray.

Heeding Billy Graham's advice and obeying God's prompting to tear down the walls that separated me from Oral Roberts was something that moved me deeply, and he and I became welded together right there. From where we had both started, it was nothing short of a miracle.

Oral then asked me to speak in chapel at the university, and I preached to the entire student body in the Mabee Center. He also invited me to speak at some gatherings of his major donors, and it seemed that God really used me when I spoke there. Through it all, Oral became one of my biggest encouragers.

My son, Randy, went to college at Oral Roberts University, majoring in media and journalism, and he met his wife there. Betty and I are so grateful for that, and for the four grandchildren we have from Randy and Debbie. Perhaps none of that would have ever happened if I hadn't been willing to go talk to Oral.

I was also able to encourage many other church leaders to get to know Oral Roberts—some of whom had been divided against him for reasons that now seem so trivial and foolish. One year we had a fabulous gathering where hundreds of preachers came just to meet with Oral and tell him they loved him. It was a wonderful experience. And God used Oral to do a deep work in my life, as well.

I went on to visit Oral many times before he died, and I remember one occasion in particular when he shared what was on his heart. It was so powerful and profound that I said to him, "Oral, the world has never really heard you. And it's tragic that the people who love you have never gotten to know who you really are inside." I regret that Oral Roberts never openly shared many of the things he said to me in private, because I think it would have had such a profound effect on the church at large. The incredible depth of his thinking, and the deep spiritual impact that God had on his life, were just remarkable.

But once people have you pegged, or have you in the place where they want you, they tend to keep you there and never let you move forward. I had a similar experience when I decided to stop doing crusades and began to focus on the television pro-gram with Betty. Some of the people who knew me best went absolutely wild. I remember Jerry Falwell saying, "James, you're the best evangelist I've ever heard. What are you doing sitting on a sofa with your wife?"

"Well, that's what God told me to do."

Jack Hayford

During that time, I also met with Jack Hayford, and we became close. The first time I visited Church on the Way, Jack took me aside in the study before I went out to preach, and said, "Your being here today is far more significant than you will ever know. This is very big in the kingdom of God."

I didn't fully understand what he meant at the time, and maybe I don't even understand the full impact now, but I was able to introduce Jack to many of my Baptist pastor friends and leaders, and they fell in love with him. They came to me and said, "Here's a Pentecostal preacher who is totally grounded in the Word of God and totally filled with the Holy Spirit, and the fruit of the Spirit is clearly evident in his life." And it began to pull down the walls that had been dividing Christians and keeping us from being open with one another.

And it wasn't just Baptists who received a fresh move of the Spirit of God. It included all kinds of conservative, mainline denominational groups, and a newfound freedom began to break out in their churches. Whether they sang traditional hymns or praise songs and choruses, they now worshiped with a greater flow of the Holy Spirit's power, and there was renewed joy and genuine love. It was as if God's family was finally beginning to respond to one another.

At one of our conferences, David Yonggi Cho, who then had the largest church in the world, came and spoke, along with Jack

Hayford, David Wilkerson, Stephen Olford, Leonard Ravenhill, and John Wimber. It was just miraculous to bring all these leaders together.

John Wimber

John Wimber was one who got turned inside out by God. I remember him saying that when he read the Bible, he wanted to go do everything in it. When he asked his friends, "Why aren't we doing all these things? Why aren't we praying for the sick? Why aren't we believing God for miracles? Why aren't we standing against demonic activity and casting out evil spirits?" they said, "Uh, we don't do that."

"Oh, so you just *talk* about it, but you don't *do* it?" he said. "I want to *do* it."

John Wimber was like a breath of fresh air for the body of Christ. And when my Baptist friends heard him—and even Catholics—they saw that he was a shining light. I was disappointed, then, when John decided to pursue the Vineyard ministry and plant some Vineyard churches, just as people were beginning to receive him everywhere. I had hoped he would keep speaking words of life to the *whole* church rather than starting another "something." If we're going to pursue unity in the body of Christ, we don't need another movement; we need a move of God on *all* movements. I'm convinced that when the church pulls together in true spiritual unity, we will see God move in even more amazing ways than what we've already seen.

When I realized that all these relationships I was building could be traced back to the time when Billy Graham said, "Spend time with people you've been taught to avoid," God really began to lead me in a miraculous stretching of wineskins to receive the greater fullness of the Spirit. I knew I didn't want to be the kind of preacher that my friend James Ryle described when he said, "Most Christian preachers are like a guy standing on a boat, blowing on his own sails. He's making a big huffing sound, but the boat's not going anywhere." And, boy, that resonated with me. I knew it was true. We need to set our sails to catch the wind of the Spirit and allow *Him* to freely move us.

Jerry Falwell

When Jerry Falwell saw that I was meeting with all these other people, he did not like the changes he saw in me. He said he thought I was a great voice for conservative views, and an effective evangelist, but he was disturbed when he saw me preaching "anywhere and everywhere."

Years later, when he and I had a moment to ourselves, he grabbed me in one of his bone-crushing bear hugs—I don't think Jerry ever realized how strong he was—and said, "James, I always thought you were the most anointed person I ever heard stand up in a coliseum or a church building, and I didn't like the changes that came when you left the big crusades and sat down in a television studio. I wasn't happy about it, but I want to tell you something." He looked me straight in the eye and said, "I want you to know that the same anointing, the same power, and the same glory that was always on you in those stadiums and coliseums and church buildings is all over you sitting there by your sweet wife on that living room sofa in that television studio. And I just needed to tell you that."

That meant the world to me. Jerry had started inviting me to preach occasionally at Thomas Road Baptist and Liberty University when I was still in my twenties, so when he let me know that he still saw Jesus in me and the power of God still at work in my life, in a way it reaffirmed that I was on the right path in reaching out beyond my own denominational walls. And as I continued to do that, I was amazed at how God brought people to me.

David Wilkerson

David Wilkerson was another person I became close to during those years of transition. I preached at some of his first Teen Challenge meetings, and he and I prayed about various things and encouraged each other. Even while he was still at Times Square Church in New York City, he would come down to his retreat center in East Texas, which wasn't far from where he was later killed in an automobile accident in 2011. I wrote a strong tribute to him after his death, and I thanked God that I could know someone like David Wilkerson.

Vance Havner

In our Baptist circles, Vance Havner was one of the greatest writers and communicators of the twentieth century. One time when he was asked how to get started as an evangelist and conference speaker, he said, "I can't tell [you] how. It just happens. God calls you, and then he'll open the doors for you to preach. He'll make a way if he's called you. You just be there."[1]

I love that. "You just be there." Yield your heart to God, and He will find you. That's how I got my start, and that's how God can use *you* in amazing ways as well.

One time when I was preaching at a state evangelism conference in Alabama, Vance Havner was sitting in the front row, weeping as I spoke on the power of the Holy Spirit. When I got to the motel that night, he stopped me on the way to my room and said, "I want you to come to my room, and I want you to lay hands on me and pray for me."

I was in my thirties; he was in his seventies.

I said, "I can't believe you're asking me to do that. *You* need to pray for *me*."

"No," he said. "I want you to pray for me."

I was humbled as that beautiful white-haired man knelt down and asked me to pray for him. And I did. When I got through, he looked at me and said, "Thank you. I want the last years of my life to be my greatest."

At that point, I dropped to my knees and said, "Sir, please pray for me." And he did. When we choose to live amazed, God will bring us opportunities to pray for, encourage, and build up one another.

> **Yield your heart to God, and He will find you. That's how I got my start, and that's how God can use you in amazing ways as well.**

Stephen Olford

Stephen Olford was at that same evangelism conference in Alabama, and I talked to him about the power of the Holy Spirit. I had heard from Billy Graham's team about an incredible move of the Holy Spirit that happened just after Dr. Olford had visited with them. They were praying in a hotel room and a mighty wind rushed so strongly in the room that one of the men got up and went to the window to see if the wind was blowing outside. It wasn't; the wind was *in* the room. Everyone present said they felt that they had received a mighty anointing of the Holy Spirit. The power and fruit of the Spirit in their lives was what had enabled the ministry to expand worldwide, and what had enabled Billy to walk with power and yet with such indescribable meekness and humility. So for someone as highly respected as Stephen Olford to be my friend and pray with me was a true blessing. Over the years I've had many encounters with people like him—people who have identified and affirmed the work God was doing in my life.

Sowing Seeds of Unity

As Christians, we need to be cautious when we're counseled to stay away from one another. Such advice is a seed of division, not unity. It is wisdom of the flesh, not the Spirit.[2] Similar issues go all the way back to New Testament times, when some of the earliest churches were in danger of being pulled apart by people taking sides in favor of one leader or another: "When one says, 'I am of Paul,' and another, 'I am of Apollos,' are you not mere men?"[3]

Here you had two great evangelists and teachers—Apollos and Paul, who were both clearly anointed and gifted by God—and yet the church was arguing about whom they favored. The people were making celebrities out of leaders who were gifted to communicate truth to the church—seed planters and waterers—and ignoring the fact that "God was causing the growth."[4] Paul finally said, "I could not address you as people who live by the Spirit but as people who are still worldly—mere infants in Christ."[5]

In Galatians 5, Paul writes that we have been set free to *live* by the Spirit and to *walk* by the Spirit; and when we *walk* by the Spirit, our lives will overflow with the *fruit* of the Spirit—namely, love, joy, peace, patience, kindness, goodness, faithfulness, gentleness, and self-control.[6] But we're not walking in freedom when we become dissentious, filled with strife and animosity, creating division and disputes among us. Those things are listed in Galatians 5 alongside all the moral improprieties that we would all agree are sinful: immorality, impurity, sensuality, idolatry, sorcery, and drunkenness, among others.[7] We saw it in Paul's day and we see it in ours: people claim to be defending truth and yet the fruit of their lives proves otherwise. They aren't walking in the Holy Spirit. A tree is known by its fruit.

I believe that people who have watched me and listened to me over the years would agree that I've never abandoned a single biblical principle I've held. I've never moved away from a biblical standard. I speak caution and correction to people in all parts of the body, and normally they will hear me and often heed what I say. I believe that's because I haven't isolated myself from them, and because we've chosen to build our relationship on the things that bring us together, not the things that might drive us apart.

Anyone who spends time with me will know two things: I love people, and I love whatever person I'm talking to. And together we're going to love the people who God the Father loves. Moreover, we don't have time to sit around and identify all the reasons why we might disagree. They're too numerous. No married couple has ever stayed married because they agreed on every issue. We all learn how to get along with our differences while preserving the essential unity and integrity of our relationships. And the same applies to our relationships in the body of Christ. But we should never compromise foundation stones and principles that are irrefutable. I'm *not* going to move away from the Word of God. And I *will not* compromise one word of truth. If you can find one place in my life that doesn't line up with the Word of God, I will get down on my knees and repent right now. I will stand on God's Word, but I'm not going to twist it to fit some traditional perspective.

> I love people, and I love whatever person I'm talking to. And together we're going to love the people who God the Father loves.

The truth is historically confirmed and established, and godly principles are as sound as the foundation that Jesus said we're to build our lives on. When we build our lives on the Rock that is Jesus Christ, it enables us to build in such a way that our lives will withstand the storms—even the storms of spending time with and talking to people who might (heaven forbid) disagree with us. But the foundation stones of our Christian faith are as clear, obvious, and irrefutable as the law of gravity and the law of aerodynamics. When we build on the Rock, it is amazing what can happen.

When I go to other people, perhaps to share a concern with them, I oftentimes see Jesus in them so clearly that I find myself corrected by their spirit, by their demeanor, and by things I'm able to witness in their lives. And if we find a point of tension, or holy friction, if we'll allow iron to sharpen iron, we will both go away keener and sharper—with greater love and greater understanding.

No one will ever persuade me to move away from biblical truth or principles. And I will continue to caution people if I believe they are compromising truth or doing something unwise. But as the Lord puts it on my heart, I will also continue to meet with people who may not agree with me on every last jot and tittle.

For example, some people have criticized me for spending time with Glenn Beck, who is a Mormon. Well, I've seen Glenn take some powerful stands on his television program. He has also recommended some important books on his show—books such as *Sacred Fire*, for example, a fabulous treatise about George Washington. I read *Bonhoeffer*, by Eric Metaxas, in part because of what Glenn Beck said about it on TV. So when Glenn invited me, along with a group of evangelical preachers, to meet with him, I went.

When we were there that day, I said to Glenn, "You know, the Lord is using an alcoholic, defeated, set-free-from-addiction Mormon to say more things of prophetic truth to America than he is with many of the preachers—even ones sitting in this room. And God may be using you to help wake us up."

As Glenn and I have become friends, we have visited with each other a lot and prayed together. I have asked him about his relationship with Jesus. Glenn has talked about a personal encounter and relationship with Christ and what Jesus has done in his life. And even though I believe that so much of what the Mormons teach seems to lead people away from the truth that Jesus Christ is the living Lord and Savior and the only way to the Father, it seems apparent to me that Glenn has encountered Jesus.

I believe Glenn's respect and appreciation for Mormons comes from the fact that they brought him to repentance and helped him find deliverance from alcohol, other addictions, and other problems. It's no surprise that he lives with a spirit of gratitude for that. Glenn has also come to Gateway Church in Southlake, Texas, many times and has heard great speakers such as Ravi Zacharias. I encouraged Glenn to talk to Ravi, and the two of them met after the service when Ravi spoke.

The bottom line is that we don't write off anybody as beyond the transforming power of God to bring them into a greater understanding of the truth and a more meaningful and personal relationship with Jesus. As mainline evangelicals, we obviously don't agree with Mormon teachings, but does that mean we cut off all ties with Mormons?

A friend of mine who spoke at Brigham Young University, and poured out his heart to the students there, told me later that it was one of the most meaningful experiences of his life. Afterward, some of the students came up to him and said, "You're the first evangelical Christian we've heard who we feel loves us and cares about us. We've always felt that many evangelicals disliked us and wanted to make fun of us."

My friend said it really touched his heart to see how the love of God had moved them. And he hadn't compromised the message one bit.

Sometimes our greatest compromise as human beings is that we don't walk in love or speak the truth in love. We don't give iron the opportunity to be sharpened by the necessary friction of other iron; we just avoid all contact.

If we disagree with others in the body of Christ, we act as if that's reason enough to get as far away from them as possible—to build a fortress around our own understanding of Scripture and begin firing verbal bombs in defense of our position. That's not the kind of "city set on a hill" that Jesus envisioned.[8]

I refuse to compromise, and I refuse to walk in any spirit other than the spirit of love. Love never fails. I want to be filled with courage, compassion, and love that are equal to my convictions. I believe I've been moved by God in a positive direction, and I'm not going to endorse, embrace, or encourage anything that violates or runs contrary to the principles of truth and the foundation stones found in the Word of God. But at the same time, I understand the undeniable power of speaking truth in love.

I've been amazed that people who don't understand why I would talk to Glenn Beck seem to have enough confidence in my desire to please the Lord and walk according to His will that they have at least accepted with graciousness and kindness what I'm doing. And if they're concerned about me, they've been kind enough to pray for me or ask me about it and give me a chance to answer.

I'm encouraged to see that God's love can lift us above the unnecessary, sometimes foolish, and often damaging barriers we have put up in our attempts to protect "sacred truth," which often is simply our own perspective being taught as the command of God. But even if we're talking about issues of absolute truth, if we will remain yielded clay in the hands of the Potter, He will shape us into vessels of honor.

If we will put our lives into God's hands, all the pressure we feel, which is intended to shape Christ in us, will either come from or be filtered through the fingers of God. God's purpose is always to *form the image of Christ in us*. Our great and faithful Father knows how to shape vessels that will honor Him and give Him glory.

When God really began to get ahold of the clay of my life and found me with a more yielded spirit, I believe I became much easier to mold—by God and by friends, critics, and even enemies. Whatever is thrown my way—even if it is harsh, unkind, mean, malicious, or coming from known enemies—I still take it to the Lord and ask Him if He's trying to teach me something. *Are these thoughts Your thoughts, Lord? How do I hear them, how do I respond to them, and what can I learn from them?* I want meekness, yieldedness, and teachableness to characterize my life. Don't you?

What the Bible Says about
LIVING AMAZED

Coming to his hometown, he began teaching the people in their synagogue, and they were amazed. "Where did this man get this wisdom and these miraculous powers?"

Matthew 13:54 NIV

They were on the road going up to Jerusalem, and Jesus was walking on ahead of them; and they were amazed, and those who followed were fearful.

Mark 10:32

6

God's Amazing Healing

Immediately the girl arose and walked, for she was twelve years of age. And they were overcome with great amazement.

Mark 5:42 NKJV

LONG BEFORE I ever began to fellowship with charismatics, I had an experience of being instantly healed of a pretty serious illness. And I mean *instantly*.

When I was in my early twenties and hadn't been preaching for very long, I developed some masses of tissue, like tumors, in my chest. They were painful enough that it hurt to even touch my chest, and the doctors said it would take some serious surgery to remove them.

One night I was preaching at a Baptist church and the musician was a Pentecostal. As we were talking before the service began, I told him about my health problems and my concerns about undergoing surgery.

He said, "You know, I believe that God heals today, just like he did in the New Testament. And I've seen him heal a lot of people. You said you're concerned about having surgery. Well, I've seen God miraculously heal things like this. Would you let me pray for you?"

I said, "Sure." What could it hurt, right?

He laid his hands on me and started praying, and then he started praying in another language. I had never heard anyone speak in tongues before, but it didn't sound strange to me. There was something angelic about it. He prayed for a minute or two, and then we went on with the evening. I preached, and he did the special music.

Later that night, when I got home, I realized that my chest didn't hurt anymore. When I went for a checkup, the tumors were completely gone. I had been healed. It wasn't like maybe something happened; it was complete and undeniable—there was *nothing left* of the tumors. I can't adequately express how miraculous this was. Two very serious, indescribably painful masses in my chest were now 100 percent gone. And there was no more pain. I had been told by two or three doctors that those masses would be a recurring problem in my life, but it has now been more than fifty years and they have never come back. Not once.

God's Healing Power

Even after that firsthand experience, I had no room in my Baptist theology for a ministry of healing. Even when I was sick with a variety of chronic ailments for a full decade of my crusade ministry, it never occurred to me to seek healing prayer. For ten years, I had terrible, persistent infections in my throat and sinuses, as well as a stomach disorder, and there were times when every functioning gland in my body that I could identify ached and throbbed with pain. But that was just the way I lived. I believed that God *could* heal me, if He chose to; but like so many

Christians today, I didn't think God necessarily *wanted* to heal me. I assumed that my nagging illnesses were just my cross to bear. In fact, I preached some of the most unscriptural messages you would ever want to hear about how healing is not at the forefront of God's mind. Some of those messages are on tape, and when I hear them now, it's like listening to a verbal assault on the very word, nature, and character of almighty God—all in the name of deep convictions in the religious realm.

And then God gloriously intervened, speaking to me through a pastor I had been warned to stay away from. Some people close to me had labeled this pastor's ministry and had told me to avoid him, which is what we do—we label things we don't understand. This was at a time when the fullness movement was first gaining traction among Southern Baptists, and my crusade director and some others said to me, "You ought to attend one of these conferences."

I decided to go to Dothan, Alabama, where a Baptist pastor named Jim Hylton was preaching on healing. We had set an attendance record for the football stadium in Dothan when we had a crusade there, and now I was going back to sit in on a Bible conference because I had heard so much about it.

Hylton was preaching from Romans 8 on the differences between the mind-set of the Spirit and the mind-set of the flesh, and he talked about watching God heal people miraculously. "Why do you want to live sick and defeated?" he asked.

When he got to verse 11, it hit me like a ton of bricks.

> If the Spirit of Him who raised Jesus from the dead dwells in you, He who raised Christ Jesus from the dead will also give life to your mortal bodies through His Spirit who dwells in you.

As the pastor read those words, I didn't hear *his* voice, I heard *God's* voice: "The same power that raised Jesus from the grave—that power lives in *you*."

As I sat in the front row at that conference, God Almighty came upon me and healed me right there. It was miraculous, instantaneous, and complete. I can't explain it. All I know is that I got well, and all those ailments never came back. Am I saying I've never had a sore throat since? No, but it has never been like it used to be.

> As the pastor read those words, I didn't hear his voice, I heard God's voice: "The same power that raised Jesus from the grave—that power lives in you."

I went home from the conference excited and refreshed and immediately prayed with Betty, who had also suffered from various illnesses for years. And she was healed.

And then God healed our daughter Rhonda, who had struggled off and on with asthma for seventeen years. During her entire childhood, she had been limited in her ability to run or play strenuously like other kids. I can still remember the last attack she had like it was yesterday. She was on the sofa in our den and was so overcome by coughing, wheezing, and shortness of breath that I thought she might choke to death. I looked across the room at her, and in the name of Jesus, I rebuked her asthma. As quickly as you could flip on a light, my daughter was healed—right in the midst of one of the most severe asthma attacks I had ever seen her have. And the asthma was no longer a problem. She went from not being able to run at all to running several miles a day.

A similar kind of healing happened with my son, Randy, who had been suffering from chronic stomach ailments for twelve years. After Betty and I showed him Psalm 107:19–20—"They cried out to the LORD in their trouble; he saved them out of their distresses. He sent His word and healed them, and delivered them from their destructions"—Randy went off alone with his Bible and prayed, and God healed him.

Many people today look for healing in the wrong place. They're seeking it at the hands of other people, rather than by the Word of God. The living Word still lives; deliverance by mere mortals is in vain.

The Healing Flow

After those experiences, I knew that healing was real and began to study the Word of God on the subject. And I became zealous for what God said. In fact, I became so caught up in the truth of God's Word that I could no longer hear the doubts and skepticism of other people—their vain speculations, assertions, and fruitless discussions.

For the next six months, *everyone* I prayed for was healed—*instantly*. I do not recall a single time, place, or occurrence, either in person or by telephone, where someone I prayed with for healing was not instantaneously healed of whatever sickness or disease they had. There were people who were dying, or waiting to die, and God healed them. The miracles were absolutely incredible. And during those six months, the thought never entered my mind that the people I prayed for might not get well. I could hear only God.

I'm convinced that God *wants* us to *live* in that reality. That's how Jesus lived, and Jesus Himself said, "He who believes in Me, the works that I do, he will do also; and greater works than these he will do; because I go to the Father."[1] But here's the problem: as soon as God begins to move in a particular way, we either want to box it, brand it, and exalt it improperly, or we want to deny the reality of it because it falls outside the realm of our understanding. But as Jesus also said, "We speak of what we know and testify of what we have seen, and you do not accept our testimony. If I told you earthly things and you do not believe, how will you believe if I tell you heavenly things?"[2]

John Wimber once said to me, "You can't get a lock on what God does. It's not a formula. You can't put it in a box." And, boy, that has really resonated with me.

God will not fit a formula—there's no formula for healing; there's no formula for miracles. It's just God. He wants us to live in total dependence on Him.

As I said, for six months, the healing was continuous. But as word began to get out, I was bombarded with requests for prayer. One day, as I was sitting in my office, the Lord said to me, "What you're seeing, this continual flow, will not continue. The day of the superstars is over. The day of the *somebodies* is over. It's the day of the Body." In other words, the entire body of Christ is supposed to be doing the work, not just one person or one ministry. This was the very thing that God had shown me when I first met with Oral Roberts.

> If people think we can obtain healing through a gifted person, rather than through the Person from whom all healing flows, then we have not advanced in our faith the way we must.

"The flow will not continue," the Lord said, "because you would not even be able to walk into this office if it did." This word was accompanied by a vision of extension ladders banging up against the outside walls of my office and people breaking out the windows and thrusting children through the opening for me to pray for them.

If people think we can obtain healing through a gifted person, rather than through *the* Person from whom all healing flows, then we have not advanced in our faith the way we must. Our trust must be in God alone, and the church must learn how to function as a healthy body.

Keep in mind that many things can limit the flow of God's healing power, and we shouldn't be quick to place blame. When

Jesus came to His hometown and began teaching in the synagogue, the people were amazed by His wisdom and power.[3] And yet the Bible says, "He did not do many miracles there because of their unbelief."[4]

So even Jesus Christ Himself—the Son of God, the King of Kings, the Lord of Lords, the One to whom all power in heaven and on earth was given—did not do many great works in certain places "because of their unbelief."

Corporate unbelief does not affect the *reality* of God's power, but it can hinder the *flow* of God's power and the fulfillment of His purpose—not ultimately, but in certain situations. Unbelief can reside in the heart of the crowd or the individual, but we mustn't waste time accusing others. We simply proclaim the truth in love, and with conviction, and leave the results in God's hands.

Severed at the Head

One time when I was ministering in Alabama, a young woman at the meeting was lying on a gurney, attached to several pieces of medical equipment. It was obvious she couldn't move. When I got up to preach, I looked at her and said, "Honey, I don't know you, but I know you came here because you know that when Jesus passes by, He does what only He can do, and I know you want to be healed. And I'm going to come over after I minister to the people, and we're going pray with you."

I found out later that her name was Kim Lunsford. Two years earlier, as a twenty-year-old college student, she had been in an automobile accident that had killed her friend. Her spine had been severed at the first and second vertebrae, leaving her a quadriplegic.

After the meeting, I went over, along with Betty and two of my associates, and knelt down next to Kim. I could see that her hands had curled in toward the wrist from atrophy. I reached down and took her hands in mine, and as I did, a desire welled up in me to see this young girl healed. I prayed, "God, heal this girl. I rebuke the destruction of her body, I rebuke the effects of her injury, and I rebuke paralysis."

I spoke healing and vitality and strength into every fiber of her body, but as I held her hand, I felt no quickening of the muscles. So I said it again: "Jesus, heal her body."

I believe that when we're living in the reality of God's ability and desire to heal and we don't see the miracles that we're hoping for, God will often tell us why. Not always in that moment, but I believe He will show us His greater purpose if we ask Him to open our eyes.

As I knelt next to Kim Lunsford that night, longing in my heart to see her get up from the gurney, I prayed, "Speak to me, Jesus." And as real as I've ever sensed anything, it was as if Jesus Himself, right there before thousands of people, knelt down beside me, put His hand on my shoulder, and said, "James, *her* hands are like *My* hands. In proportion to what they're supposed to be, *My* hands are like *her* hands. Her body is like My body on earth today—*severed at the head.* Kim understands the condition of My body, and Kim is an intercessor for the healing of My body. As My body is restored, her body will be restored. Tell her that."

When I told Kim what the Lord had said to me, she nodded. Two days before the conference, she had told her mother that Jesus had spoken those exact words to her. Again, like so many things I've witnessed over the past thirty-plus years, I can't explain it apart from God's miraculous and supernatural intervention.

Kim Lunsford's body never was healed in this life. After that conference, she lived for another seventeen years, to the age of thirty-nine, and by all accounts her life was a testimony to God's faithfulness. In a news article at the time of her death in 2000, it was reported that "Kim's strong belief in God's purpose for her and her deep faith gave her strength and hope. Although she was a quadriplegic and spoke with the aid of a mechanical device, she was an inspiration to people, young and old, as she went about speaking at churches and giving her testimony of faith."[5]

A Proven and Tested Faith

I've never known anyone with more faith in God's ability to heal than our daughter Robin had. And during the course of her life, she experienced some tremendous healing.

When she was eleven years old, she developed a terrible growth on her lip that soon became quite alarming. It was a bulbous, tumorous mass, about the size of the tip of my pinkie, and it was ugly—like a cigarette ash hanging from the corner of her lower lip. Robin could barely brush her teeth or eat.

Betty and I prayed for her, and we had everyone we knew pray for her, but the growth didn't go away. If anything, it got uglier. And of course everyone would stare at Robin when she walked into a room. If she hadn't had a pretty strong disposition and character and been pretty secure in who she was, it would have been tough on her. But she handled it well.

We took Robin to our family doctor, but he said he couldn't remove the growth. He sent her to an oral surgeon, who told us it would be difficult to remove the growth without leaving a noticeable scar. He referred us to a plastic surgeon.

When Betty took Robin in for a consultation, the plastic surgeon said he could do it, but it would require specialized surgery and would be several weeks before he would have the time available.

I was out of town at the time, at one of my crusades, and when I called and Betty told me about the delay, I was upset. We didn't understand what the growth was or why it didn't go away, and now the surgeon was saying Robin would have to live with it for another month.

While I was talking to Betty about her conversation with the plastic surgeon, Robin asked to speak to me. When Betty handed her the phone, Robin said, "Daddy, I know why the doctor didn't do it. God told me that *He* wants to be the one to heal my lip."

On the following Sunday night, Betty had a dream that the growth had fallen off into Robin's hand during the night and she was healed. Betty got up and checked on Robin, but the growth was still there. The next morning, Betty told Robin about the dream: "I had a dream that you walked into our bedroom with that thing in your hand, saying, 'Look, Mom. Look what Jesus did. He healed me.'"

Robin had a role in the school play at the end of the week, and she said to Betty, "Momma, I don't want that thing on my lip when I get up there on Friday night."

On Monday, while Robin was taking a bath, Betty heard her talking in the tub. She stopped and listened at the door for a minute and then stepped into the bathroom and asked Robin what she was talking about.

"I was just practicing my testimony," Robin said. "We have chapel on Friday, and I'm going to tell the whole school how Jesus healed my lip."

Betty walked away thinking, *Oh my goodness, she's really taking my dream seriously.*

By midweek, the growth was still clinging to Robin's lip, and by Thursday night, it was worse than ever.

That evening, we all went to Randy's Little League game, and Dudley Hall, one of my associates, was there with his son. He said that when he saw the growth on Robin's lip, he cringed with pain. When he went home that night, he gathered his family and they prayed for Robin.

I left the house on Thursday night, right after the ball game, and drove to East Texas for a directors' meeting that would begin the next day. I got in at one o'clock in the morning.

At five o'clock, the telephone rang. When I picked up the receiver, Betty was on the other end and she was as fired up as I have ever heard her.

"James," she said, "we've been waiting an hour to call you, and we've been shouting all over this house. At four o'clock this morning, Robin got up, and that thing was in her hand! Her lip is healed! It is perfect! I can't believe it. It's a miracle!"

When Robin walked into the bedroom with the growth now resting in her hand, Betty immediately looked at her lip to see if there was any visible damage. Because the growth was so deeply rooted, the doctor had said it would take intricate, precise stitches to keep from leaving a noticeable scar. But all Betty could see was a spot the size of a pinprick.

Laying On Hands and Praying

I believe God sometimes allows illness or injury when He wants to stretch our faith and teach us more about His character and goodness. I've seen this many times in my own life and in the lives of my friends.

Johnny Cash and I were close friends for many years before his death in 2003, and we often prayed together during challenging times. I remember him calling me after his son, John Carter, who is the same age as my son, Randy, was involved in a jeep accident when he was a child.

I said, "Where are you right now?"

"I'm standing at the foot of the bed," Johnny said. "I'm looking at my son, and I don't know if he's going to live."

"Johnny," I replied, "I want you to walk around to where you can reach John Carter, and I want you to lay your hands on his chest somewhere."

This was at a time when I had recently seen God do a lot of miracles. I hadn't really prayed for those miracles; I had prayed more "if it be Thy will, heal him" types of prayers, but God had taught me some things about His heart and His desires.

As a parent, do you want your child to be sick or in pain? Of course not. So how can we argue that God, our loving heavenly Father, doesn't want us to be healed and healthy? Think about it: If God *wants* us to be sick, why do we go to the doctor to try to get well? If we don't believe that God *wants* people who are sick or hurt to be healed or get well, should we be paying doctors and other health professionals to go against God's will, risking their lives and their futures by fighting against Him?

Can God use sickness and suffering to accomplish His purpose? Absolutely. Can God use pain? Yes, pain can be our friend when it alerts us to a problem. But don't we also take action to alleviate that pain?

I've learned to pray with an active faith, believing not only that God is able to heal but also that He likes to heal. And because we want Him to heal us, we should not hesitate to ask Him to heal us. And let's trust Him to do what's best.

> I've learned to pray with an active faith, believing not only that God is able to heal but also that He likes to heal. And because we want Him to heal us, we should not hesitate to ask Him to heal us. And let's trust Him to do what's best.

The New Testament gives us many examples of the laying on of hands to impart healing, gifts, and blessing.[6] Jesus did it. The disciples did it, and they anointed people with oil. But in our day and age, I remember some of my friends and others making fun of those who laid hands on people.

Now, we're not to make an *idol* out of the laying on of hands; we're not to put a serpent on a pole and worship it, but we ought to do what God has instructed us to do. Like John Wimber said,

"Let's do the stuff." Let's do what God said, let's not just talk about it. Let's not just discuss it. *Let's do it.*

I said to Johnny Cash that day, "Go lay your hands on your son, and we're going to pray for him." And God saw fit to heal John Carter and restore him to health. It was a wonderful affirmation of God's faithfulness, mercy, and grace—and our faith was refreshed and renewed.

A Big Buck, a Bad Back, and a Beautiful Testimony

One day, about twenty years ago, I got a call from my friend John Morgan, the longtime pastor of Sagemont Church in the greater Houston area.

"I know you've been hunting some property that has tremendous wildlife," he said. "I'm calling on behalf of Andy Pettitte, who really wants to go deer hunting. He's never seen any really big deer."

"Who's Andy Pettitte?" I asked. I wasn't a big baseball fan, and this was early in Andy's career.

"He's the winningest pitcher in the American League over the past two seasons, James. He's a local boy, from Deer Park, still in his early twenties, and he plays for the Yankees. He'd like to know if you'd take him hunting."

"I'd be glad to," I said.

So Andy came out and stayed in a little trailer that Betty and I had on the property. It wasn't the Ritz-Carlton, but he was happy to be there. We had a nice deer stand on a tower more than twenty feet high, so you could see a long way across the South Texas brushland. I've never seen anyone who enjoyed watching the wildlife more than Andy Pettitte. I told him we had seen a large, mature buck recently and maybe he'd come by again.

Sure enough, one morning the buck started coming our way. I saw an opening in the brush, about two hundred yards away, where I thought we might get a shot. I told Andy, "If the deer comes to that opening there, that's where you need to take him, because I don't know if you'll get another chance."

Andy had his rifle positioned and ready to shoot, and we could tell that the buck was headed toward the opening.

As the buck drew near, Andy started shaking so hard that he was vibrating the chair that *I* was sitting on. He had buck fever worse than anyone I've ever seen. I looked him in the eye and said, "You're the winningest pitcher in the American League?"

He just grinned and kept shaking.

When the buck stepped into that opening, I have never seen anyone go from shaking like a leaf to being so calm, so still, and so perfect as Andy Pettitte. And he made the perfect shot. It was incredible.

But that's not even the highlight of the story.

While we were sitting in the deer blind that morning, Andy said, "James, I hurt my back recently, and it could jeopardize the beginning of my season. I hope you'll pray for me."

That night we talked about the power of God to heal and got down on our knees in that modest little trailer—me at six foot three and Andy at six foot five—and we asked God to heal Andy's back. His church in Deer Park, Central Baptist, was also praying for him, as one of their favorite sons and husband of the pastor's daughter.

Well, God healed Andy, and he went on to pitch very successfully in the major leagues until he was forty-one years old. He holds the all-time Major League Baseball record for postseason starts (42), innings pitched (263), and wins (19).

Even that isn't the highlight of the story.

Andy has always been a little shy, but he came on our television program in March 2001 to give his testimony and to tell people about the miracle that God had worked in his life. He also invited the members of his church, who had prayed for him so faithfully, to come up from Deer Park (a nearly five-hour drive to Dallas) to be in the studio audience. After Andy gave his testimony on *LIFE Today*, more than seven hundred people called in to give their lives to Christ, many of them from the New York City area. I don't think I've ever seen anybody more thrilled than Andy was when I told him that.

When Healing Doesn't Happen

More than twenty years after Robin was healed of the growth on her lip, she was diagnosed with throat cancer. Now in her early thirties, with a husband and three kids, she was active and beloved at her church, and her tremendous faith was once again on display. During a seven-year off-and-on battle with the disease, she never feared, never complained, never doubted. She just knew she'd be made well. In fact, she signed every email with "I win." And yet, on December 28, 2012, surrounded by her family, Robin died.

So what happened?

Did her faith fail?

No. I've never met anyone with faith quite like Robin's.

Did Betty's or my faith fail?

No. We never wavered in our hope or belief in God's miraculous healing power.

Do I understand why my daughter died of throat cancer?

No. She had never smoked or used tobacco in any form.

Did it make any sense at all?

No.

When her eldest son got engaged recently, I knew she would have loved to help plan everything for his wedding. Robin was the greatest celebrator on the planet. But she's not here.

Could her death have destroyed our faith?

If we had put our faith in anything other than God alone, then yes, it might have. But God is our fortress and our shield. We don't understand, but we trust.

Without question, God could have healed Robin—right up until the moment when she stepped through into eternity. He can do anything. But can God also, through the loss of our precious daughter, help us to bind up more broken hearts because our own hearts have been shattered? I pray He does, because that's what Betty and I want to do, and our hearts have certainly been broken. And all the people who cared for us and wept with us—they helped to bind up our hearts.

I went to a funeral the other day for a longtime friend, and I thanked God for the blessing of a building filled with people whose lives had been affected by the Christlike witness of this person's well-lived life. And that's how it was with Robin. Her husband and their three children are living amazed—rejoicing over her life, rather than dwelling on her battle with cancer and their loss. Though they miss her greatly, and always will, they look with anticipation to see the eternal impact of the fruit that will spring up from the seeds she sowed by her life *and* her death. And, as an evangelist, I don't want *anybody* to miss for themselves what Robin saw when she walked up into the portals of heaven.

Losing our daughter hasn't changed my view of God's miraculous healing—or my belief in God's desire to see people healed and made whole. You wouldn't believe the number of people I've met in just the last year who had the same disease Robin had but are now 100 percent cured. And a lot of them don't seem to have any faith at all. Our healing lies in the *object* of our faith—almighty God—not in the size or strength of our faith. But I don't want to get into any nit-picking, hairsplitting arguments about the intersection of our faith and God's healing power. The quicker we lay aside those pointless disputes and simply confess that we don't understand—but we trust—the more we will see God do miraculous things.

God is all-powerful, all-merciful, and all-loving. He is sovereign over everything, including life and death. We know He is the same yesterday, today, and forever. He healed yesterday, He heals today, and He will still be healing tomorrow. It's not a formula we can package, but it is a living reality we can see and experience. We can live with an *active* faith, not a passive if-it-be-Thy-will resignation.

God always has the final word, but we should be praying *boldly* for the sick and the suffering. We should be *asking* God to perform miracles. We should be *trusting* Him for His mercy, wisdom, and grace. And if we don't see the miracles we're praying for, we can still trust God for the miracle that enables us to walk in peace, hope, and faith, even with the pain that accompanies loss. From the seeds of our own pain, we will grow hearts of compassion for others and bind up their broken hearts. That's what it means to live amazed.

What the Bible Says about
LIVING AMAZED

He got up and immediately picked up the pallet and went out in the sight of everyone, so that they were all amazed and were glorifying God.

Mark 2:12

People were overwhelmed with amazement. "He has done everything well," they said. "He even makes the deaf hear and the mute speak."

Mark 7:37 NIV

Jesus rebuked the unclean spirit, and healed the boy and gave him back to his father. And they were all amazed at the greatness of God.

Luke 9:42–43

7

God's Amazing Heart for the Lost

Immediately, when the entire crowd saw Him, they
were amazed and began running up to greet Him.

Mark 9:15

WE HELD A CRUSADE one year in Sulphur Springs, Texas, and if
you would have asked me at the time, I would have said it was
one of the most difficult places I had ever preached. The community seemed complacent, indifferent, and divided. But then
I heard a story that left me living amazed and reinforced for me
the truth that God doesn't make mistakes, God isn't constrained
by "difficult places," and God can work through anyone who is
yielded to him.

A young woman in Sulphur Springs named Sue had lost her
nephew in an automobile accident. One evening she ran into
Clark, the younger brother of a friend of hers, and he reminded
Sue of her nephew. Feeling guilty that she had never talked to her
nephew about Jesus, she decided to make up for it by witnessing

to Clark. He seemed unimpressed with what she shared with him, but Sue decided she wasn't going to give up.

When our crusade came to town, Sue decided that Clark had to be there. So she went to work on him, inviting him repeatedly throughout the week. Clark was a hard nut to crack, but by Friday Sue had gotten him to agree to go with her to the final night of the crusade on Saturday.

Clark had grown up with an abusive father and both parents addicted to the bottle. He'd had no exposure to religion of any kind, and he didn't know the first thing about it. But he showed up at the crusade on Saturday night.

When I preached that night, I told part of my story of having grown up without a father, and how when my father finally did come around, he was an abusive alcoholic. Something about what I shared got through to Clark, and when I gave the invitation, he came forward and one of our volunteers led him to the Lord.

Sue was overjoyed. She told Clark that he had to go to church with her the next morning and also get baptized. When he went home and told his mother what had happened and said he was going to church the next day, she asked if she could go with him. So, on Sunday morning, Clark, his mother, and three of his sisters went to church for the first time in their lives—and all four women went forward at the invitation. Clark, who had been a Christian for less than twenty-four hours, led his mother in the same prayer he'd been taught the night before, and she was set free from a lifetime of alcoholic addiction. She never took another drink, and within a year she was leading a Bible study at the church Sue had invited them to. Clark himself went on to become a pastor—his name is Clark Whitten, and he's the founding

> I want to see every person come to know God the way I've come to know Him.

pastor of Grace Church Orlando and a longtime friend of mine. One year, while serving a church in New Mexico, he led the Southern Baptist Convention in number of baptisms performed.

Restaurant Witness

During one of our crusades one year, we stayed at the same hotel as the Gaither Vocal Band, who were in town to do a concert at a different venue. In the lobby one night, as I was on my way to go preach, one of the Gaither singers came up to me and said, "Do you remember meeting me years ago at a Howard Johnson's restaurant in Florida? I was kind of a hippie type, and I was sitting there in a booth, with a bandanna around my head and was all strung out, and you came over to the table and said, 'I just want to talk to you for a minute.' And you sat there and shared Christ with me. Do you remember that?"

I said, "You know what? I *do* remember that."

"James, I gave my life to Jesus when you walked away that day," he said. "Now I'm in Bill Gaither's band. I'm one of his lead musicians, and we have a show tonight."

That encounter, and dozens just like it that I've had over the years, resulted from one simple fact: I have the love of God in my heart for every person I meet, and I want to see every person come to know God the way I've come to know Him.

That's why, in churches packed to overflowing, in stadiums and coliseums, when people saw a man up on the platform with perspiration flowing down his face, moving about with zeal, they knew that he loved them. And they knew he was trying to deliver something to them that would make their lives better—now and forever. *They knew it.* And they would listen.

And that's why I've been able to walk into any football locker room, high school gymnasium, biker club meeting, nightclub, civic club, social club, country club, restaurant, café, or truck stop and ask people for a minute of their time. And as soon as I open my mouth, they know I love them and that they're listening to someone who, with all his heart, wants the best for them.

A Life-Changing Walk

In 1975, a young man named Peter Jenkins was walking across America and writing an article about his journey for *National Geographic.* One Friday night, in Mobile, Alabama, he was on his way to a wild party he'd heard about when he saw a number of billboards advertising our crusade in town that week. He had his camera with him, and being from upstate New York, he was curious to know what a so-called Southern holy roller revival meeting might look like. By his own account, he was expecting to find a "striped tent" filled with "sawdust, ignorant people, and screaming preachers."[1] What he found instead was a city auditorium packed with ten to twelve thousand people.

Unable to find a seat, he came all the way to the front and found a spot on the floor near the foot of the platform. When I stepped up to the podium, I saw this long-haired kid with a great big camera, complete with autowinder and telephoto lens, taking pictures of me from the edge of the platform while I preached.

As I completed my message and prepared to give the invitation for people to come to Christ, this kid's camera was so noisy, and he was such a distraction, that I was mentally preparing to rebuke him and tell him to stop taking all those pictures. But before I could say a word, the Lord stopped me in my tracks and said, *Don't say a word. Leave him alone.* And I did.

Hundreds of people were now coming forward, and when I looked down at the young man again, I saw he was no longer taking pictures. Instead, the camera was hanging by its strap around his neck and tears were rolling down his cheeks. Peter himself describes it in his book *A Walk Across America*:

> With all these thousands of men, women, and children, the place became as quiet as the deep woods. An awesome hush fell over everyone. I bowed my head, trying to pull myself together. . . .
>
> I was afraid for James Robison to ask his final question of the night. I was trying desperately to be rational, yet I felt out of control and helpless. I had never been so moved. This was the last place on earth I expected such a thing to happen. . . .
>
> The deepest corners of my being were lit with thousand-watt light bulbs. It was as if God himself were looking into my soul, through all my excuses, my dark secrets. All of me was exposed to God's searchlight. . . .
>
> I was realistic and sober when James Robison asked us to repeat a prayer with him. I heard myself saying, "Lord Jesus, I want the gift of eternal life. I am a sinner and have been trusting myself. Right now I renounce my confidence in myself and put my trust in Thee". . . .
>
> We all finished our request to God, and my next sensation was beyond the words of the world. A vibration shot from the top of my head to the bottom of my feet, like a current of pure truth pushing out the old Peter and putting in a new me. It still seemed too simple. But I felt clearer, cleaner, and different from ever before in my life. Something transforming had happened to me here.[2]

Peter's story in *National Geographic* was the first time, and probably the only time, the magazine ran an article that clearly pointed people to Christ and the way of salvation. Accompanying the article was a picture of the closing night of the crusade at Ladd Stadium in Mobile, with more than thirty-five thousand people in attendance.

Johnny Cash and June Carter joined me that night, with their entire group. That was also the night a disabled girl was brought out from an ambulance on a stretcher and gave her testimony. When she finished by saying, "The angels are coming. Jesus is sending the angels to come and get me and take me to heaven," Johnny Cash just about lost it up on the platform. Those words were a powerful reminder to him of the death of his brother, Jack, at the age of fourteen, an event that marked the course of Johnny's life.

I had heard the story of Jack's death from Mama Cash, Johnny and Jack's mother, one time when I had met with her. Johnny had told me that I was his mother's favorite preacher and that she had wanted him to be my singer, but I told her, "I think Johnny'd be better off doing what he's doing. He can win people to Jesus right where he is."

Mama Cash told me that when Johnny was about twelve, he had tried to convince his brother to go fishing with him one day. Instead, Jack went to work in the shop at the school, making fence posts to earn some money. While he was working, he accidently leaned in to a circular saw, which instantly cut through his sternum and sliced through his esophagus and his intestines. I don't recall how Jack got to the hospital, but the next time Johnny saw his brother, Jack was lying in a hospital bed, unable to eat or drink. Jack's mouth was so dry that he kept asking for water. Mama Cash said they would put a wet cloth up to his mouth to moisten it, and Johnny later told me that in his mind's eye, he saw the image of Jesus on the cross asking for water.

It was a matter of days before Jack succumbed to his injuries, and Mama and Johnny were both there with him. Right before he passed, Jack suddenly looked up in the corner of the room and said, "Do you see 'em? Do you see 'em?"

"See what, son?" Mama Cash said.

"Oh, Mama, don't you see 'em? Don't you see 'em?"

"What, son? What?"

"The angels, Mama. Look at the angels. They're coming to get me."

Johnny never forgot that day, and in many ways it haunted him until he died, contributing to his addiction to prescription drugs and alcohol. And he never forgot that his brother had wanted to be a preacher, which was why it weighed heavily on him when his mother told him he should do the crusades with me.

That young woman's testimony on our final night in Mobile hit Johnny full force, and it was a powerful experience for everyone. After she spoke, I hardly had to give an invitation before hundreds of people began streaming forward to receive Christ.

Peter Jenkins reported on the magnitude of the crusade's effect, including how God moved people's hearts and how his own life was changed. He has since written other bestselling books, and there's no question his life was miraculously changed that night.

A Transformation That Money Couldn't Buy

Another man whose life I saw transformed up close and personal was Cullen Davis, who in the mid-1970s became the wealthiest man to ever stand trial for murder. His trial was the longest and most expensive in Texas history at the time.[3]

Davis was an oil man and entrepreneur who was accused of wounding two people, including his estranged wife, Priscilla, and killing his twelve-year-old stepdaughter and Priscilla's boyfriend. He was acquitted at the trial but soon after was arrested again on suspicion of trying to hire a hit man to kill the judge in his divorce trial. It was endless news in Texas at the time.

During the second long trial, which also ended in an acquittal, I heard the Lord say that I was to go witness to Cullen Davis. So one Sunday evening at First Baptist Euless, where I was a member, I went up to the pulpit and said to the congregation,

"The Lord has told me I'm going to win Cullen Davis to Christ. And I need you all to pray with me."

After Cullen was acquitted, I went to see him in his office. He was from a wealthy family, and a billionaire in his own right, so when I walked in, the first thing I said was, "Sir, I'm not here because of your money, and I didn't come to talk to you about that. We trust God to take care of our needs, and He uses people who have very little. I've come here today because God loves you, and I want you to know Christ."

It really got his attention when I told him I wasn't there for his money, but for something more important. He invited Betty and me to his home—a magnificent mansion, with an Olympic-size indoor swimming pool and every luxury you could imagine, situated high on a hill on more than a hundred acres of priceless land.

Not long after we arrived, I began sharing Christ with Cullen and giving him the plan of salvation. His new wife, Karen, was there listening, along with Betty. After a time, I asked Cullen if he would like to give his life to Christ, and he said, "Well, ten minutes ago, if you would have quit talking, I would have given my life to Christ, but you kept preaching to me so I had to wait until now." And with that, he dropped down on his knees and gave his life to Christ. This was within a year of when I had asked the church to begin praying with me.

Karen Davis had two sons from a previous marriage, one of whom had some hearing issues that required special care, so they had hired a student from nearby Texas Christian University to look after the boys. We had taken our seven-year-old daughter Robin with us that day, and she was sowing seeds of life with the nanny while Betty and I were meeting with the Davises.

At one point, as she walked around that big mansion, Robin said to the nanny, "This sure is a big house."

"Yes, it is," the nanny agreed.

"But it's not near as big as God's house," Robin said.

That simple and frank statement had such an impact on the nanny that she gave her life to Jesus. She was marvelously saved and became a beautiful witness.

Even after Cullen Davis was acquitted, a lot of people in Texas still believed he was guilty as charged—and many were suspicious of, and doubted, his conversion to Christ. But perhaps the greatest testimony I heard came from a man who was close to the case and knew the particulars. He told me, "I still think Cullen Davis is guilty, but I can tell you that he's the greatest miracle I've ever seen in my life. He is a totally changed man."

An amazing transformation like that can only be attributed to the power of God.

Beating the Odds

Sometimes reaching the lost is as simple as *noticing* and *caring*—just seeing people and responding to the nudge of the Holy Spirit. In so many situations where God has used me to touch people's lives, they had no idea I was a preacher or an evangelist. I simply noticed them and reached out to them. When they saw that I noticed them, and that I cared, it overwhelmed them. And many times it changed their lives. I've seen it happen in all sorts of situations. Wherever we find people, we find people in need of Jesus.

> Sometimes reaching the lost is as simple as noticing and caring—just seeing people and responding to the nudge of the Holy Spirit.

One of the greatest miracle conversions I've ever witnessed happened on a driving range at a country club golf course. I saw a man who looked lonely and miserable, so I approached him. He turned out to be a big-time bookie with a weakness for drugs and exotic dancers. He had also helped manage some adult clubs. I started telling him about Jesus, and the next thing I knew he was praying with me, asking God for help—right there on the driving range. And it had a tremendous impact on the country club.

I found out later that other members of the club had been gambling on this guy in the clubhouse—they were actually taking bets on how many more days he would live before he self-destructed. He was weeks or days away from being dead when I led him to the Lord. But since that day twenty years ago, he's been on fire for God. In fact, he brought Stacie, one of the dancers he knew, to my office to visit with Betty and me, and we led her to Christ.

My assistant, Carol, who observed some of the changes in Stacie after her conversion, later saw her at a service I spoke at in Orlando.

"She looked like an angel," Carol said. "It's hard to believe how much she had changed."

That's what it means to live amazed and to see the power of God change the entire course of someone's life. And all because someone noticed and cared. That's something we *all* can do.

The Problem with "Face Value"

Part of what we need to get beyond is our tendency to judge people and situations based on appearances. Noticing and caring about people means getting close enough to see past the facades they may be hiding behind or the defenses they've put up to keep people at bay. Sometimes we need to reach out to people who don't look, act, think, or believe like we do. And sometimes we need to realize that what we see on the outside isn't always an accurate reflection of what's happening on the inside.

A good example would be guitarist Brian "Head" Welch of the band Korn. His full beard, long dreadlocks, and tattoos covering almost every visible inch of his body certainly make a statement, but Jesus has turned him inside out. In 2008, Brian appeared on our show to promote his book *Save Me from Myself*. He brought his nine-year-old daughter, Jennea, with him, and she came and sat in his lap as we ended our taping, creating a striking visual contrast with her dad and providing some insight into his true character. He has an amazing story—he's not perfect by any means, but Jesus's effect on his life has been remarkable.

Two days after we aired that interview, Beth Moore called me and said, "Do you realize that I sat there and watched you talking to Brian Welch—looking like he looked, and you sitting there loving him the way you loved him—and the minute that television program was over, I jumped into my car and went to the bookstore. I bought that book, and I read every bit of it that day. I did not put it down. And you cannot know what that did for me to see how you loved on him."

God sets for us the ultimate example: "People judge by outward appearance, but the Lord looks at the heart."[4]

Too often in the church we cut people off because we judge them based on one thing they do that we disagree with or that we think is inappropriate, improper, or unbiblical. When we see somebody who looks different, talks different, dresses different, or has a different understanding of something in Scripture, we make them feel condemned—not convicted, *condemned*—by our pious self-righteousness. And it keeps us from reaching them.

When we decide we don't like somebody because of something about them, we need to remind ourselves that if God took that attitude with us, none of us ever would have known His love. But God's love is big enough that Jesus forgave the very people who were deliberately killing Him—and killing Him viciously—even as He was dying on the cross.

There was nothing right about what they did to Him, and yet He said, "Father forgive them." But here we come along and write people off because they don't agree with us.

God makes it pretty clear in the New Testament that there's nothing He despises more than self-righteousness.[5] Jesus gave His sharpest rebukes to the self-righteous people who were so grateful they weren't like others.[6] Jesus said they wouldn't be justified like those who *know* they're in trouble. When we encounter people we disagree with, or whose lives we believe are off track, we should *pray* for them, not condemn them. And we should love them enough to show them a better way.

Reaching the Lost among the Found

Sometimes the people who most need an encounter with Jesus have been hearing about Him their entire lives. And God may choose to work through us as His chosen vessels to break through to them.

In 1984, Rick Gage was a twenty-five-year-old assistant football coach at Texas Tech University. He was also the son of Freddie Gage, a well-known Southern Baptist evangelist. Although he had come from "a Christian home, a great ministry, and great churches," he hadn't realized that he "didn't have the real thing."[7]

> Sometimes the people who most need an encounter with Jesus have been hearing about Him their entire lives.

When Rick heard I was preaching at a church in Lubbock, he decided to come hear me because I had played catch and other games with him and his brother when they were kids.

When he arrived, the place was packed, and he sat in the very back to my left. When I gave the invitation, this son of a well-known evangelist was under such conviction that he came forward and gave his life to Christ—and he was absolutely transformed. It was miraculous.

"For the first time in my life," he said, "the Bible became real to me. I stayed up until three in the morning, reading my dust-covered Bible, where the words were jumping off the pages into my heart. I fell in love with the Author of the Bible, and His words became life to my soul."[8]

Suddenly, a preacher's kid became a child of the living God. He has gone on to become a great evangelist, and he's still on fire for God and going strong, preaching citywide crusades in small communities across the nation. He's doing in small stadiums what Billy Graham did in larger venues. Rick's organization, GO TELL Ministries, also puts on great youth camps.

The Night the Football Team Got Saved

About a year after I graduated from high school, I went back to Pasadena to preach during the month of July. Frank Hale, who was the starting halfback on the football team, came to one of the first meetings and got right with the Lord.

Afterward, Frank approached me and said, "Hey, James, I gotta get the football team to come hear you. I'm gonna go get all of 'em."

"Are y'all practicing already?" I asked.

"No, not yet," he said, "but I know where they all are."

So Frank went to all the pool halls and fast food places, everywhere kids hung out, and got more than half of the Pasadena High School football team to come to the next meeting. One of the kids he brought was George "Buddy" Cheshire, an incredibly talented football player and track athlete, who went on to become a top receiver at Baylor.

Frank found Buddy Cheshire at the pool hall and said, "You're coming to this church, Southside Baptist, and you're going to hear James Robison preach. He used to be on the football team here."

Buddy said, "I'm not coming."

"No, you're going to come," Frank said, "or I'm going to whip you. I'm not kidding. Everybody else is coming, and you better be there."

Buddy told Frank he'd be there, but then went and bought a case of beer and iced it down in the trunk of his car. His plan was to sit through the meeting, to make Frank happy, and then invite all the guys to go down to Galveston, about seventy miles away on the Gulf Coast, to hang out on the beach and get drunk.

At the meeting, Buddy found a seat about a third of the way back on the left side of the sanctuary. While I was preaching that night, I started seeing little pieces of fuzz floating up in the air over by where he was sitting. Apparently, Buddy's athletic socks had some loose fabric that he could pull on, and he was making little fuzz balls and blowing them up into the air.

Before long, they were floating everywhere, and about half the crowd was watching them. Meanwhile, I was preaching on the power of sin—how it fascinates, but then it assassinates.

Buddy sent up fuzz balls during the entire service, until I gave the invitation. He later told me, "At that moment, I just froze, and God jumped all over me."

Maybe two or three people had come forward when, all of a sudden, Buddy leapt to his feet, shoved everyone between his seat and the end of the row out into the aisle, almost knocking them all down in the process, and came running to the front of the sanctuary. In one smooth leap, he was up on the platform, and with a mighty stiff-arm like the great receiver and kick returner he was, he shoved me away from the pulpit.

Grabbing the sides of the pulpit with both hands, he said to the congregation, "Listen to me! I came here to ruin this meeting. I've got a case of beer in my trunk, and I came here to get all the football players to go down to Galveston with me and get drunk. But I got Jesus! And Jesus got me! And if you don't get up out of your seat and come down here right now and give your life to Jesus, you're the biggest fool that ever lived."

With that, he jumped off the platform as every football player in the building, and many other people, came streaming forward to accept Christ. It was like a cattle stampede, and about half the football team got saved that night.

Bucking the Trends

One football player who had helped Frank Hale get the team to show up at that meeting was quarterback Rick Carlisle. He was a wonderful kid who was already a Christian.

At the end of the school year, Rick and his girlfriend, Kathy Thurman, were voted Mr. and Mrs. Pasadena High School. It was customary for the winning couple to be crowned at the senior prom, but Rick and Kathy, who later married each other, announced to the school—I think it was even over the PA system—that they were not going to the prom. Instead of going to the dance, which as young, conservative Christians they saw as compromising, they wanted to have a nice banquet instead.

When school officials told them they were required to be at the prom in order to be crowned as Mr. and Mrs. Pasadena High School, they said, "We're not going. You can take away the honor and even kick us out of school, but we're not going to the prom."

The matter was eventually put to a vote and the students voted to have the banquet. It became a tradition and consistently attracted more students than the prom.

When I told that story at subsequent crusades, many other schools started holding year-end banquets as well. Rather than providing a traditional prom dance for kids who would typically go out and party before and after, the schools would bring in an inspirational speaker and have a nice dinner for everyone to enjoy.

In our contemporary culture, it may sound silly for a group of students to say, "We don't dance," but the point I'm trying to make is that there was a zeal for God that was so great that these kids were willing to go against the trends. What kind of move of God would it take today for people to go against the trends in our country? We need that kind of move desperately. The way the lower courts and Supreme Court now attack religious freedom, an inspirational speaker may one day not be allowed within a mile of our children.

Redeemed and Redeployed

Sammy Tippit, an atheist who was named "Most Outstanding Youth Speaker in North America" at a United Nations conference in 1964, came to our 1965 crusade in Baton Rouge to make fun of the revival. Instead, he was radically born again and went on to become a worldwide evangelist. He became known as "God's Secret Agent" for his work in Eastern Europe before the collapse of the Soviet Union, and God used him powerfully in Romania, even before the revolution. In more recent years, he has been remarkably effective working in Africa and the Middle East and now has a daily gospel outreach in Iran.

Another young man who came to hear me preach in Baton Rouge was David Stockwell, a gifted athlete who went on to play football at Rice University and became active in Fellowship of Christian Athletes. A self-described troublemaker as a kid, David became a great evangelist after being born again and has won many people to Christ through his evangelistic ministry.

Shaking His Fist in the Face of God

Willie George first heard me speak at MacArthur High School in Irving, Texas, when he was a student there. His football coach had come to a crusade meeting, and after hearing me preach, he had told his players, "I encourage you to go hear James Robison tonight."

With the coach leaning on him to attend our meeting, Willie came that night to see what was happening. But even though he fell under conviction during my message, he wasn't ready to come forward. At the end of the service, as I was closing the invitation, he remembers hearing me say, "You don't say no to God politely. You're either going to surrender your life to Christ or you're going to clench your fist in the face of God and say, 'It's *my* life; I'll live it like I want to!'"

"Boy, when I walked out," Willie told me later, "I knew I had my fist in the face of God—every moment. I could feel it with every step I took."

Willie said he couldn't sleep that night, and when he got to school the next day, he told the other football players, "I'm going back to hear James Robison tonight, and when he gives the invitation, I'll be the first one down that aisle." And sure enough he was.

Willie George got saved that night and soon became a youth pastor at a church in West Texas. From there he went on to do some great outreach to young people. For several years in the 1980s, he aired a children's television program called *The Gospel Bill Show*, in which he played the part of a cowboy and used animals effectively to teach Bible lessons to kids.

In 1987, he founded Church on the Move in Tulsa, Oklahoma, which now has an attendance upwards of ten thousand people each week. As part of the church's outreach to young people, he built an old Western town called Dry Gulch USA, complete with a narrow-gauge railroad with little steam locomotives and railcars for kids to ride around the Dry Gulch property. The town, which has waterslides and plenty of wildlife for kids to see, hosts summer camps and retreats that minister to thousands of people every year. During the Christmas season, the church uses the railroad for The Christmas Train, which takes passengers through a depiction of the Christmas story and attracts as many as fifty thousand riders during the holidays.

God has also used Willie to equip youth leaders working all over the world, and the impact of his ministry over the past thirty years has been tremendous. Willie was also pastor to our precious daughter Robin, her husband, Ken, and their children. All three of the kids now work on staff at Church on the Move. The oldest, Chris, was just named head baseball coach for Lincoln Christian School, the private school that Pastor Willie started.

Pressing On

People have come to me over the years and said, "James, you say that so-and-so was saved at one of your crusades, but look at him now. He's making a mess of things." Whenever I hear of people who are struggling, or when I'm facing temptation in my own life, I'm reminded that the walk of faith is a lifelong journey, and we have an enemy who is constantly working to knock us off course. That's why it's so important for the body of Christ to be united and to encourage one another.

> We'll never get away from the fact that we're all sinners in need of a Savior, in need of the sanctification and work of God's grace in us continually.

We'll never get away from the fact that we're all sinners in need of a Savior, in need of the sanctification and work of God's grace in us continually. I'll never forget one morning when I was meditating on Scripture and the Lord spoke to me as clearly as if He were sitting right next to me. He said, "I use imperfect people to accomplish my perfect will. I always have and I always will."

The people mentioned in this book are not perfect. We're not talking about people who haven't failed or who won't fail. But we *are* talking about the one Person who doesn't fail, and who will never fail us, even though we fail Him. We may walk away from God, but He will never walk away from us.

We will never earn the grace that God is willing to pour out *on* us and *through* us—a grace that must never be described as cheap, because it was purchased at a great price. That price included the separation of Jesus from His Father and indescribable agony, even beyond that which could be seen. It included physical torture through the beating, the scourging, the mockery, the thorns on His brow, the spikes in His hands and feet, and the spear through His side—and even more so through the pain in his heart as He took on the weight of all our sin. Jesus died not from suffocation, the typical cause of death for those who were crucified. He died literally of a broken heart. The weight of our sin caused His heart to rupture, to explode within His chest.

When we see all that Christ has done for us and realize that He will never leave or forsake us, we can rest assured that He will kneel down and offer us His listening ear while extending His saving hand to us in any pit we find ourselves in—however deep and whatever its origin. It matters not to Him if we fell in, were thrown in, or dug the pit with our own misdeeds, rebellion, and sin. In grace and mercy, He offers to lift us up and establish our lives on the solid rock of His love and truth.

The spirit of the enemy is deceptive and destructive, but the Spirit of God is redemptive—always working to reconcile and restore. Even when we are far from God by our own foolish choices, He still waits for every prodigal to come around the bend in the road so He can rush to them and cover them with the love that has never failed and never will fail. Whether we have yet to come to Him or we have stumbled along the pathway of faith, God never expresses disappointment in us. Instead, he is disappointed *for* us when we fall short of His best intentions for us because of our own wayward foolishness.

God has always used imperfect people to accomplish His perfect purpose—which never justifies sin or evil, but which speaks to God's relentlessly redemptive nature. The Bible is filled with examples of imperfect people, and the Bible never whitewashes its characters; it tells us exactly who they are. If you look at the lineage of Jesus, you'll find not only a prostitute but also a murderer and an adulterer. And it's those kinds of people—sinners like you and me—that God uses to present Christ to the world.

But even if we are obviously imperfect people, when we speak perfect truth, in perfect love, gospel truth can transform the most imperfect person. So we press on and faithfully run the race that God has set before us.

What the Bible Says about
LIVING AMAZED

They were all amazed, so that they debated among themselves, saying, "What is this? A new teaching with authority! He commands even the unclean spirits, and they obey Him."

Mark 1:27

Jesus, looking around, said to His disciples, "How hard it will be for those who are wealthy to enter the kingdom of God!" The disciples were amazed at His words.

Mark 10:23–24

Jesus said to them, "I did one miracle, and you are all amazed. . . . Stop judging by mere appearances, but instead judge correctly."

John 7:21, 24 NIV

8

God's Amazing Provision

Amazement had seized [Simon Peter] and all his companions because of the catch of fish which they had taken.

Luke 5:9

THE PRINCIPLES OF GOD and the freedom he offers through the truth—and through the Person who *is* the Truth—are so great and so highly effective when put into practice, that we must experience the power of gospel truth or quickly make idols of the blessings and benefits that freedom offers.

I believe the lessons I learned from my experiences growing up in poverty are important for our nation today. I was poor and had no inside track to employment or anything else. But I always worked, and nothing could stop me from achieving. I'm also thankful that my mother never made me think that I needed the government to take care of me or that somebody owed me something.

If I had been taught during my formative years that somebody else should take care of me or that they would take care of me, I don't think I ever would have made it out of poverty. I would have become just another defeated person living in dependence on the government. Instead, I looked out from the mire and the misery of my impoverished situation, and I saw possibilities and opportunities. I saw hope and potential. And I was willing to work hard to make the most of myself and my situation.

I never resented people who had what I didn't have. Never. Nobody taught me to hate people who had something more than I had. And I think that's very important, because bitterness and hatred and believing that other people owe you something are the most sure and rapid ways to wind up in bondage to a system of learned helplessness and dependence.

Even though my mother rarely had two nickels to rub together, she taught me a strong work ethic. And I can guarantee that even if I had never met God, I would have succeeded by the world's standards because I would have worked hard regardless and taken advantage of the opportunities I uncovered along the way. Nobody twisted my thinking to where I thought others were supposed to take care of me. American freedom gave me a chance to do anything I wanted to do and become whatever I wanted to become, and I was determined to be a winner.

Learning to Work

I started working when I was twelve, and I don't even like to hear the arguments today about minimum wage. I went to work for forty cents an hour, and I worked really hard. Some say that twelve years old is too young to work, but it wasn't for me. I got a job sacking groceries and stocking shelves in a grocery store, and within six months, I was overseeing every department except meat. I wasn't given a formal title, but I had a tremendous amount of responsibility. I took care of produce and dairy and managed all the stocking.

I was still twelve years old and had been working there for not quite a year when the manager said to me, "James, I've never known anybody like you. When you grow up, you could probably manage a store like this."

However, my twelve-year-old brain thought, *No, when I grow up, I can own a store like this.*

Even as a little boy, I saw opportunity in the land of the free and the home of the brave. I wouldn't listen to the limitations that other people tried to put on me. Oh how I wish people would hear that same truth today. I wish we would get rid of the limitations that foolish, excessive government places on people—limitations that hinder initiative, vision, and hope and foster laziness, dependence, and despair. We must refocus the role of government as primarily *protector*, not *provider*. Uncle Sam must never be presented or perceived as Father God.

I want to see compassion rise up among people in our nation, because without a compassionate connection between one another, no amount of money can heal the hurts and ills in our society. When you hand something to someone out of a misplaced and misappropriated sense of obligation, guilt, or pity, and then don't require any accountability for how those resources are used, you're asking for exactly what we have today: a dependent class of socially immobile people who have no hope of ever bettering their situation. We have to create opportunities, yes, but we also have to hold people responsible and accountable for doing what they need to do to better their lives. The current system merely heaps foolishness on top of foolishness, until the entire nation becomes foolish and the people who most need the help are damaged. Having come out of this kind of life myself, I know firsthand what I'm talking about.

Depending on God and God Alone

Dependence on anything other than God is a damaging, idolatrous, self-centered, greedy approach to life. It's like the Israelites selling out to Pharaoh and no longer being the productive, free people that God had intended them to be. And even after He delivered them out of Egypt, they mishandled their freedom and before long had fallen back into bondage: "They became disobedient and rebelled against You, and cast Your law behind their backs and killed Your prophets who had admonished them so that they might return to You, and they committed great blasphemies."[1]

When we put God's principles into action and do not stray from them, the fruit of righteousness we harvest is bountiful and indescribably effective. But we must never reduce the measure of God's blessing down to a monetary or material standard. Never. There's no limit to what God can do, but what He chooses to do is His business. We're never going to have a fixed formula, and we need to cast aside all false standards of measure. Some of the most blessed people I know, who without a doubt are walking in God's favor, have very little monetarily. But their lives are rich, full, and satisfying, and they know that God will take care of them. One of the biggest problems people run into when they see God do something that, in their minds, confirms what's in His Word, is that they want to build a theology around it. And then they erect a fortress to defend their particular point of view. God has made it absolutely clear to me that building walls to separate brothers and sisters in Christ from one another is a waste of time. Those walls become prison walls, and we don't need that.

One story in particular in the Old Testament illustrates an important principle for receiving God's blessing. And that same story later became an interesting backdrop to an encounter that Jesus had with the people of his hometown of Nazareth. But first the bedrock principle: *If you will seek first to meet the needs of others, God will supply everything you need.*

Jesus confirmed and expanded the borders of this principle in the Sermon on the Mount when His talk of God's provision culminated in this well-known statement: "Seek first the king-dom of God and his righteousness, and all these things will be added to you."[2]

In the Old Testament story, the prophet Elijah, who has just predicted a drought that would last for three-and-a-half years, is sent by God to Zarephath, where a widow and her son are gathering sticks to prepare their final meal before they die of starvation.[3] Elijah asks the woman for a drink of water and to prepare some bread for him before she feeds herself and her son. Despite her limited resources, she does as Elijah requests, putting his needs before her own. As a result, Elijah's promise of the Lord's provision comes true for her, and she has enough oil and flour to continue to eat for the duration of the drought.

Jesus later made an interesting reference to this story when he pointed out to the people of Nazareth that "there were many widows in Israel in the days of Elijah . . . and yet Elijah was sent to none of them, but only to Zarephath, in the land of Sidon."[4] He followed this up with the observation that "there were many lepers in Israel in the time of Elisha the prophet; and none of them was cleansed, but only Naaman the Syrian."[5] It was these remarks—simply stating the factual truth of the Old Testament—that so enraged the people of Nazareth that they attempted to drive Jesus off a cliff outside of town.

> If we make it a priority to meet the needs of others, even when it seems prohibitively costly, God will take care of us.

What can we learn about God's amazing provision from these two stories? If we make it a priority to meet the needs of others, even when it seems prohibitively costly, God will take care of us. He will meet our needs. And when we seek to follow the Lord's leading and meet the needs of those He puts in our path—often in supernatural ways—others in the church may rise up to resist and condemn our faith and our actions. They may even become angry and try to cast us down. But we must follow the Lord's leading and do what He calls us to do, even if we don't completely understand it.

The Water of Life and the Day of Harvest

Jesus made a habit of associating with people who his disciples—and everyone observing Him—thought he should avoid: lepers, tax collectors, and people who didn't know the right way to worship.

A startling and thought-provoking moment in the New Testament occurs when Jesus meets the woman at the well in Samaria. This is also the longest recorded conversation that Jesus has with anyone in the Gospels. It's a familiar story for many: Jesus was out of place, sitting at a well outside a Samaritan city at noontime, talking to a woman who had come to draw water. By all cultural standards of the day, it was inappropriate and unacceptable for a Jew—much less a Jewish rabbi—to speak to an unmarried woman who had led a promiscuous life. But Jesus saw her real need—with prophetic accuracy—and He offered her the one thing that would make a difference: the living water of faith in God.

"If you only knew the gift God has for you and who you are speaking to, you would ask me, and I would give you living water. . . . Those who drink the water I give will never be thirsty again. It becomes a fresh, bubbling spring within them, giving them eternal life."[6]

The woman asks about the proper place for worship, but Jesus asserts that it isn't the *place* that matters—it's the Person we worship who matters. He said, "The day is coming when they will worship Me in spirit and in truth." Sometimes I wonder if we're still waiting for that day, because we get so caught up in the traditions of men, dissension, and division, and we feed it, support it, and defend it—all inappropriately.

Jesus tore down traditional beliefs and practices, and His obvious love and concern for this woman affected her so deeply that when she left, she went back into town, where her life had been one of shame and sorrow, and told everyone, "'Come and see a man who told me everything I ever did! Could he possibly be the Messiah?' So the people came streaming from the village to see him."[7] With perfect peace and confidence, the woman gave her testimony in the village, knowing that she was completely covered by God's love. As Peter writes in 1 Peter 4:8, "Love covers a multitude of sins," and it never exposes another person's vulnerability or weakness through self-righteous motivation.

Recently, as I studied this passage in John 4 again, I saw something I'd never seen before. When the disciples came back to Jesus and were amazed to find Him speaking to the Samaritan woman, their main concern was that it was time to eat. "Let's not be concerned about people's lives, their past or future, their need of forgiveness, redemption, and a new life, a new way, and a new beginning. We want to talk about food!"

Jesus said, "I have food to eat that you do not know about. . . . My food is to do the will of Him who sent Me and to accomplish His work."[8]

When we talk about God's provision, we get so wrapped up in material blessings—what we're going to eat, what we're going to wear, where we're going to live, how where we live demonstrates God's favor on us—that we so easily read right over all the passages in the New Testament that say, "Don't worry about that stuff; focus on what is important to God."

When the disciples started talking about food, Jesus said, "Lift up your eyes and look on the fields, that they are white for harvest. Already he who reaps is receiving wages and is gathering fruit for life eternal; so that he who sows and he who reaps may rejoice together."[9]

Farmers say that when the fields are white for harvest, it means we must move quickly because the time is short and we must not miss the opportunity. Jesus wasn't pointing to a field of grain, He was referring to all the people who were drawn by the Samaritan woman's testimony and were streaming from the village to see Jesus.

The Lord has shown me several times recently that we're not to waste our time on unfertile soil—not when there are fields white for harvest. "Look around," He says. "There are people everywhere just like the woman at the well. People with real needs. People who need to *hear* the gospel and *feel* the love of God. People who are thirsty for the living water of the Spirit. People who are ready to receive and experience the amazing joy of being released into God's care—that wellspring of love, peace, and freedom. Everywhere you look, there's another tax collector up in a tree; another seeker; another lost, confused, downtrodden sojourner who is feeling hopeless, helpless, unloved, overlooked, and unimportant."

As Jesus, in his mind's eye, scanned the "fields" of souls that were ready for the harvest, I believe He saw hundreds of women like the one He had just met at the well. And I think he saw thousands of men like the ones she had been with. Everywhere you look, somebody is waiting for an encounter with the living Holy Spirit of God. If we don't experience the transforming power of the gospel that gives us new hearts and new minds, all the material blessings in the world are nothing but sawdust. However, when we experience the transforming power of the gospel, even the bad things that happen, even the pain

> If we don't experience the transforming power of the gospel that gives us new hearts and new minds, all the material blessings in the world are nothing but sawdust.

we must endure, God uses to develop something valuable and meaningful in our lives.

God's Provision When We Put Other People First

From the time we were first married, Betty and I have never gone into debt, even though we started out making only $6,000 of combined income our first year. We've always been committed to living below our means, so that we would always have the freedom to be generous and would never be caught in the snare of indebtedness.

Even as kids, we thought ahead to what we might need to save for. With all the demands of the crusade ministry, we knew we were going to need a place to go for relaxation and restoration. So we started thinking in terms of a lake house or cabin, a place of escape where we could fish or see some wildlife, and we bought furniture that we knew we could move into our little getaway. It ended up being a mobile home, a very small one, but it served our purposes for several years.

As the ministry grew, I began to establish relationships with businesspeople and ranchers, and they would occasionally invite Betty and me to make use of their property for hunting. I saw an opportunity to bring groups together for hunting leases, and the landowners appreciated the fact that I always brought in high-quality people who respected the property, didn't drink, and left the property better than they found it.

At one point, the Briscoe family—one-time Texas governor Dolph Briscoe Jr. and his son, Chip—placed an ad to lease one of their ranch properties, and an attorney friend of mine contacted them. We put together a hunting group, and I soon had an opportunity to inspire proper wildlife management on Briscoe Ranch, which is the largest single-family-owned ranch in the state of Texas at more than six hundred thousand acres. The Briscoes were buying ranches everywhere in the state to accumulate the hundreds of thousands of acres they wound up with.

I got to know Chip, who had recently graduated from college, and as we began to hunt on his family's property, it didn't take long for me to realize that they were root plowing brush and clearing it on every ranch they bought, to the detriment of their wildlife habitat.

I told Chip, "You're ruining your future. You're destroying your fawning cover and the brush where the quail and other birds build their nests."

He said, "Well, the cattle can't eat that brush."

"Yes, but the wildlife will prove to be more valuable than the cattle, and you're destroying their habitat."

At first, he didn't want to hear it, but I kept after him. Still, it took me fifteen or twenty years to help convince the Briscoes to quit root plowing and clearing all of South Texas to create grazing land. Finally, one day Chip called me and said, "You're right. My dad and I think those deer are worth more than the cows, so would you come talk to us about what we can do to make it better?"

Because I had an interest in that sort of thing and had studied it, I was able to encourage them to checkerboard their clearings or leave large strips of brushland where the quail and other birds could nest and the fawns could find cover. Preserving some brushland for the wildlife enhanced the hunting value of the land, which became a much more reliable source of income than cattle ranching, which rises and falls with the ever-fluctuating price of beef.

My motivation for helping the Briscoes was not to see what I could get out of it. I was happy to help them recognize the value in what they had and to stop damaging it. By showing an interest in them and what they were trying to accomplish, I was able to speak life into the situation. And I try to be that way with everybody—my heart's desire is to help people in any way I can.

When I was seven or eight years old and living on a piece of property that bordered a junkyard, I didn't have a nice place to live or play. So I played in the dirt, building ranches with little stick fences and corrals and buildings. I had some plastic horses and cows, and I'd put them all over my little ranches, and when my friends would come by they thought it was amazing.

I've even built little ranches out behind our house with some of my grandkids. Even with all the game consoles and other electronic distractions, they liked to play in the dirt with little stick fences and plastic farm animals when they were young. I believe that God looked down on me when I was a little boy playing in the dirt, making the best of my circumstances. He said, "That little boy likes ranches." And even though ranching didn't become my life, my interest in livestock and wildlife enabled me to bless others—which ended up blessing Betty and me. In other words, God the Father was interested in *me*, and in my interests, and I believe He is interested in *everyone*, if they'd just realize it. But the key is getting interested in what *God* is interested in, with the same zeal to live for the sake of the kingdom. It's amazing what happens when we focus intently on the Father's dreams and desires.

When the Lord put it on our hearts to live below our means, it opened up a lot of opportunities that Betty and I would otherwise never have been able to consider. If someone needed help with their business or simply needed prayer, I did my best to give them wise counsel and never asked for or sought any kind of return or compensation. Being motivated to help others, we've been able to take on a servant role, enabling us to help people get close to and better hear God. Betty and I have never given a gift with a focus on the return. We've never given our children or grandchildren gifts hoping or expecting they would give us something because of it. We give to give, and bless to bless, because blessing others is an indescribably great blessing in itself.

God put a love for people in my heart. And even though many things in people's lives may need to be adjusted, and even though I may not agree with many things that people do or say, I'm still able to deliver to them the message of God's love. Working with people because we care about them, not because of what we might get out of it, opens up all kinds of opportunities to be used by God and receive God's provision. When we focus first on doing things God's way, it is amazing how other things fall into place. That doesn't mean we won't have challenges; it doesn't mean we won't have some setbacks; but it does mean we will learn the meaning of God's promise: "My grace is sufficient for you, for power is perfected in weakness."[10]

What the Bible Says about
LIVING AMAZED

All who heard Him were amazed at His understanding and His answers.

Luke 2:47

"We hear them declaring the wonders of God in our own tongues!" Amazed and perplexed, they asked one another, "What does this mean?"

Acts 2:11–12 NIV

9

God's Amazing Hand on History

All who heard it were amazed at what the shepherds
said to them. But Mary treasured up all these things
and pondered them in her heart.

Luke 2:18–19 NIV

As MY MINISTRY gained its footing in the 1960s and people began
to see what we were doing, church leaders and congregations
were not the only ones who took notice. The gifting that God
placed on me to preach caught the attention of some major business leaders in my home state of Texas—and in nearby Arkansas.

When I was in my early twenties, I came to the attention of
H. L. Hunt, who at the time had the highest net worth of any
individual in the world, and J. K. Wadley, who had made his
fortune in lumber, rail transportation, and oil.

One day, when I was twenty-three years old, I received a
phone call from a man who simply said, "Would you meet me?
I've worked with J. K. Wadley, who is an oil magnate like H. L.

Hunt, and I'd like to meet with you to discuss some things." I sensed that this man was very wealthy.

At the time, I didn't know who J. K. Wadley was—and we didn't have the internet for online searching—but, as a Texan, I knew H. L. Hunt was the richest man in the world. This caller was dropping names like crazy, but I agreed to meet with him.

When we got together, he told me he had observed my speaking ability and had seen how people responded to me. Consequently, he wanted to take me under his wing, teach me the oil leasing business, and have me present oil deals to potential investors. He had everything lined out; all I had to do was present the deals and we would make a fortune.

He promised to pay me an enormous sum of money and give me a bunch of oil stock. He also agreed to buy me everything I needed to do the presentations. He bought me the most expensive suits and shoes at Neiman Marcus—he bought me the most expensive *everything*, and all of it was tailor-made. I'd go in and get measured and they would custom-fit everything for me. When you consider how I had grown up, this was absolutely overwhelming.

The next thing I knew, Mr. Wadley also wanted to get to know me and help me. I found out along the way that he had chartered the Wadley Blood Bank and had endowed some buildings at Baylor University. He was a great man, and we got along wonderfully. But as I began to work with Mr. Wadley and his partner, I lost my peace with God.

When I told them I could not continue with what they wanted, and gave everything back, Mr. Wadley accepted my decision, but his partner was quite unhappy with me. I wish I still had the handwritten letter from him, addressed to "The World's Biggest Fool." The first sentence read, "You *think* you just gave up a lot of money. You don't have any idea what you just did." Maybe not, but I got back my peace with God. That's far more important than any offer or promise from mortal man.

The Plan

During this time I was doing crusades all around Dallas and preaching at First Baptist Dallas every off Sunday. One day I got a call at my house, and when I picked up the phone, the voice at the other end said, "James, this is H. L. Hunt."

My stomach dropped down into my shoes. H. L. Hunt was unequivocally, unquestionably the richest man in the world at that time. He was Bill Gates and Warren Buffett all wrapped into one. He said, "I've been following you for two years. I've heard you every time you've preached at First Baptist, and I've heard you at places where you wouldn't have even known I was there. You're the greatest communicator I've ever seen in my life. I'm calling to ask if you would come to my home. My wife and daughters want to meet you, and I'd like to talk to you."

I went to Mr. Hunt's estate at White Rock Lake, and after meeting his wife and teenage daughters and eating an unbelievable meal, I sat down with Mr. Hunt in his office, just the two of us.

He looked at me from across the desk and said, "This nation is in serious trouble, James, and I have a plan to turn things around. I want to make you the president of an independent oil company and begin to teach you what you need to know. I know you're young, but I know what I'm doing.

"Next, I want to put you on the radio. I've never heard anyone who can communicate quite like you. I have a team of research people, and you will be the most knowledgeable person out there. You're going to know more about national issues than anybody alive. I know you are conservative and you will not compromise. And that's why I'm willing to tell you that I'll put everything I have behind what I'm talking to you about."

At this point, I had no idea what he was talking about, but he soon laid out his plan for me.

"If we work this right, and we will, you will be elected president of the United States in 1980, and at thirty-six years old, you will be the youngest president in American history. The youngest and the most conservative."

He showed me a notebook with all the details, and it was truly impressive.

"But the reason I called you and brought you here tonight," he said, "is the same reason I'm afraid you're going to make me sad. I don't think there's enough money in the world to convince you to accept my proposal. And that's what concerns me. I'm afraid that the very thing that drew me to you—the strength of your convictions—may be the reason you turn me down."

I was feeling a little weak in the knees, but I looked back at Mr. Hunt and said, "Sir, I don't even know how to tell you how I feel right now. I'm shaking to hear you talk like this to me. But I believe if I step down from being a preacher and stop preaching the gospel and doing what God called me to do, it would be the biggest mistake I could ever make."

I could tell he was disappointed, but he heard me out.

"It's an incredible plan. And you've certainly got the money to back it up, but I can't do what you ask. You see, I believe that if I do what God has called me to do, I will have more impact on this country than I would have if I were president. I think that the job of a preacher is the highest office that a person can hold. So it's no sacrifice to me to say no to what you've proposed. It's not even difficult for me to say no. It would be difficult to say yes."

As he absorbed my response, it was as if all the air had gone out of him. But I knew I was making the right decision. There wasn't a doubt in my mind. And let me make it clear for anyone who might think, *Boy, that was a great sacrifice James made.* There are plenty of things that have distracted me over the years, but my heart has *never* gone after money or fame. *Ever.* Resisting a chocolate brownie might be a challenge. Or key lime pie. But money has never had a pull on me. I don't have a problem *with* it, or *without* it. So, for me, walking out on that deal was no more difficult than saying I didn't want to eat a plateful of dirt. It was just that simple. I was convinced—and still am—that my life would have a greater impact if I did what God had called me to do.

The Prayer Meeting That Helped Save Freedom

Though H. L. Hunt would not live to see it, in 1980 the nation did indeed elect the most conservative president of the twentieth century—and one of the most conservative in US history. But he was the *oldest*, not the youngest, to ever serve. And the role God allowed me to play in the election of Ronald Reagan is another example of living amazed.

One day in 1979, I got a call from Bill Bright, the founder of Campus Crusade for Christ. He said, "Billy Graham asked me to call you, James, and invite you to a prayer meeting we're organizing. Billy wants us to pray for two days, and he would like to see if you can get Charles Stanley and Adrian Rogers to come. Billy and I have rented an entire floor of a hotel so we can pray without distraction. And we've chosen a place near the Dallas-Fort Worth airport, because it's centrally located."

Bill Bright went on to explain that Billy Graham had been in Red Square, in Moscow, and had seen the obvious and excessive military buildup taking place in the Soviet Union. God had spoken to his heart and said, "Unless America has a change of direction and a great change in leadership, you have a thousand days of freedom left."

Sometime not long after that, and unbeknown to either man, Bill Bright himself was in Moscow, and he heard the same thing from the Lord: "Unless there is a change of direction in America, freedom's future is over." Bill too sensed that there was a time frame of a thousand days, or about three years.

When Bill and Billy later spoke to each other and discovered they both had heard the exact same thing in the exact same place, they were motivated to take action. This prayer meeting they were proposing was the result of that conversation.

While Bill was calling me, Billy was calling Pat Robertson of *The 700 Club* and Rex Humbard, whose *Cathedral of Tomorrow* television program appeared on more stations than any other program during the 1970s.[1] Billy's brother-in-law, Clayton Bell, would also participate, but he wasn't able to stay for the whole time.

I agreed to call Adrian Rogers, who was then the president of the Southern Baptist Convention (SBC), and Charles Stanley, pastor of First Baptist Church of Atlanta, who would later serve in the same role.

"Can I bring my pastor, Jimmy Draper?" I asked. "We're close, and he will be president of the SBC in the near future. I think it would mean a lot for him to be in this meeting."

Bill said, "Let me check with Billy."

Not long after, he called back and said, "Bring your pastor." Adrian and Charles also agreed to come, and on the appointed day, we all convened at the hotel.

When I spoke to Jimmy Draper recently and asked him what he recalled about the prayer meeting, he said, "I remember how serious we all were. Everything was absolutely solemn. We had an overwhelming sense of our need for God, and we all realized that unless God did something, there was nothing we could do. By the time it was over, I think we all felt that we had become part of something that God just took over."

Jimmy's memories of those two days brought back to my mind the immediate and unmistakable sense of the Holy Spirit's presence in that room when we first walked in. I remember sitting at the middle of a big, wide rectangular table and hearing Billy

Graham unload his heart about the issues facing our nation and the message from the Lord he had sensed while in Moscow. Bill Bright confirmed his own sense of being led by God and said, "We have to have great leadership in America right now, and we don't have it. The leadership we have in our nation cannot handle what is about to come at us. We *have* to have a great leader, and one who can communicate with the American people and tell them the truth."

Billy said, "I find myself wondering if this Hollywood actor—the former governor of California—might be that person."

At the time, Ronald Reagan hadn't announced yet that he was going to run. In fact, he had implied to the people closest to him—people like Jerry Naylor, his good friend and national director of special events—that he *wasn't* going to run.

Some animosity toward Reagan simmered within the Republican Party because he had run against Gerald Ford, the incumbent president, in the 1976 primary.

"Am I crazy?" Billy asked.

"I just have to tell you all," Bill Bright said, "that we *both know* what we heard God say about the three years."

Coincidentally, General Daniel Graham, a former deputy director of the CIA, former director of the Defense Intelligence Agency, and at the time cochairman of the Coalition for Peace through Strength, had heard the same message from God—that unless major changes were made, the United States had only three years of freedom remaining before the Soviet Union would begin an ascendency of domination in world affairs. And all these people—Billy Graham, Bill Bright, and Daniel Graham—ended up being significant players in what transpired.

So we began our prayer meeting with this heavy load, and we realized that these men believed they had heard God *very specifically*.

Some, no doubt, will want to pick apart that last statement. Was it a word of knowledge? Was it a prophetic word? Where did it come from? Haven't those gifts passed away? How can we rely on something so subjective?

For the glory of God, let's stop the nonsense! God is the same yesterday, today, and forever. He can do whatever He wants to do, and He can use whomever He wants to use.

Here we had all these different men: Billy and me, both Southern Baptists, and Bill Bright, who came from a strong Presbyterian background. Bill didn't even believe in some spiritual gifts—especially not a prayer language—and yet I watched him totally change his views in later years. And then we had three current or future presidents of the Southern Baptist Convention—Adrian Rogers, Charles Stanley, and Jimmy Draper—along with Pentecostal preachers Pat Robertson and Rex Humbard. All of us were being stretched spiritually as we shared our hearts and came together to worship and pray.

It turned into an unbelievable prayer meeting—and I mean, we *prayed*. Other than taking breaks to eat and sleep, we prayed and sought God's direction for the next two days.

About midway through the second day, after we had been hard at prayer for the better part of the morning, Billy Graham looked at everybody all of a sudden and said, "Can I ask y'all something?"

When we had all turned our attention to him, he said, "Do any of you men feel *holy*? I mean, do you *feel holy*? Because I've got to tell you, men, I don't. I don't feel holy. I don't know if I'm a holy man."

This was an arresting moment for all of us.

"I know holy people. I think my wife, Ruth, is holy. And her parents, who are missionaries, I think they're holy. And I know some other people who I think are holy. But I don't know if I'm holy."

I remember it as clearly as if it were yesterday. Adrian Rogers let his hand fall down on the tabletop, and his head slumped forward as well.

"Billy, if you're not holy, what about all of *us*?"

We all broke into prayer with renewed vigor. I don't know that any of us grasped the fullness of holiness, but in that moment we said, "God, we want to be holy. Whatever that looks like, we want Your will, and we want what's best for this nation. And we want the church to lead an awakening." We had another incredible time of prayer, and it was quite emotional.

After the prayer time, we began to discuss next steps, but none of us knew what to do. Eventually, the question was asked, "Do you think there's any way that someone can talk to Reagan and see where he is on a decision?"

Billy said, "I've got to say something to all of you. And you may not understand this, but this is just how it is. I believe that some men, like you, need to take this matter and walk it out and just see what God wants to do. You're going to have to talk to these people, and somebody needs to talk to Reagan. *But I can't.* I can only pray. Whatever I would do publicly would backfire. I have been burned so many times by my proximity to presidents and from my relationships with political leaders. And then terrible news comes out about something in their lives. You know I had a wonderful friendship with Nixon—he came on the platform at our crusades—but I've been burned, and I've been hurt. So I can only pray."

Another fist came down on the table, and this time it was Charles Stanley's. He said, "Billy, I would give my life to turn this nation around, to see freedom saved. I will do whatever it takes."

On the other side of Billy, Adrian Rogers said, "Bless God, you know I'm a fighter. You know if I don't have a fight, I'll start one. That's just me. I'm always fighting for truth. But I'll tell you one thing: if I don't have freedom, I don't have a place to fight for what I believe is right. So, Billy, I *guarantee* I'll stand for freedom."

I strongly believe that if we get on the wrong side of what the Lord is doing, we're not going to experience his blessing. If pastors and priests fail to stand together now against the flood of evil, they will be held accountable by God. Freedom, including freedom of religion and any public witness, is under fierce assault, and we must stand together in unity.

When the question was raised about who might be able to talk to Ronald Reagan, I said I thought I might have some access. Pat Jacobson, wife of a prominent Fort Worth physician, proved to be an instrumental connection. As the Texas Republican executive committeewoman, Pat is credited with turning the entire state of Texas to a strong conservative Republican base. She had attended some of my Bible conferences and followed my ministry. Thanks to Pat's involvement, a meeting was arranged with Mr. Reagan.

When he and I met in a hotel room in Atlanta, I talked to him about Jesus and told him what Billy Graham, Bill Bright, and the other preachers had said about the potential loss of freedom. I could see that it shook him to the core, because he was trying to discern what he was supposed to do.

I said, "They feel that if you understand freedom's principles as our Founding Fathers did, and you will stand for them, you may be the man who can communicate the truth to the American people and inspire us to move back in the right direction."

Reagan was astonished to hear what these Christian leaders were saying about him, and though he didn't know me from Adam, he seemed to take my words to heart. It was shortly after this meeting that Reagan made it clear he would be running for president in 1980.

Washington for Jesus

During that same time of prayer at the hotel in Dallas, Pat Robertson had looked across the table at me at one point and said, "James, I want to ask you something. We have a Pentecostal pastor, named John Gimenez, who wants to organize a Washington for Jesus prayer meeting on the National Mall. It's Pentecostal and charismatic."

He turned and looked at Bill Bright, as well, and said, "Would the two of you consider joining with John as tri-chairmen of Washington for Jesus, and make it a total-church prayer meeting? James, maybe you can bring in these mainline Bible Baptist leaders and Southern Baptists. And, Bill, with the Campus Crusade influence, and the influence you've got all over the world, can we turn this into a real prayer meeting, for the whole body?"

I said to Bill Bright, "I'll do it if you will."

"I will," he said.

I looked at Adrian Rogers and Charles Stanley and said, "Do y'all understand our doing this?"

When they both nodded, I asked if they would speak at the meeting, and they agreed. Jimmy Draper also said he would help, and he spoke at the rally as well.

The night before the gathering on the Mall, in April 1980, I preached a service for the pastors at Constitution Hall. Maybe three thousand pastors were there, and I preached on spiritual unity and working together, which I was just beginning to learn something about. But it was a powerful message, and the whole place responded.

Washington for Jesus drew something in the neighborhood of half a million people for a prayer meeting on the National Mall. (Of course, there were differing estimates of the turnout, but based on what I saw that day compared to other gatherings on the Mall that I've seen, I'm confident the number was at least half a million.) And it was on that platform that God confirmed an idea that He had put on my heart.

About two-thirds of the way through this big prayer time, as I was looking out at all those people, I turned to one of the other pastors and said, "Look at them. They look like sheep without a shepherd. They're out here praying, and they really care about our nation. They know we need a miracle, but they don't know what to do. But I think God has shown me something we need to do."

Later, when we could speak in private, I told this same pastor my idea for a national affairs briefing. "We need to bring in some great leaders who can tell people the truth about freedom and explain some of these things. And we need to bring together church leaders."

Reagan and Deaver

As my idea for a national affairs briefing began to gain some traction with other Christian leaders, I spoke to Ronald Reagan about it, and he agreed to speak at the gathering—though not with the approval of his staff.

Reagan must have felt in his heart that he had to do it, because the people around him were strongly opposed to it. Political consultant Michael Deaver, who later served on Reagan's White House staff, chewed me out—literally cursed me out—because I had convinced Reagan to participate in the briefing. Pat Jacobson had given him a letter outlining the details of what we would cover and who would participate, and with time to consider the potential benefits of the national affairs briefing, it was not a difficult decision for Reagan. He fully agreed with what we were trying to accomplish.

When I had met with Reagan in Atlanta, I asked him whom he most admired in our nation, and he told me it was George Washington. I asked him why and we kind of teared up together because the same things in Washington's life had moved both of us.

Reagan pointed to Washington's desire to know divine Providence and God's direction, and to have spiritual wisdom. He noted that Washington hadn't sought the role of leadership he attained as president, and yet when he got it, he really tried to know the Lord's will. That had really moved Reagan.

After we had talked for a while, I said, "I need to ask you a question: Is Jesus real to you?"

He paused, lowered his head, and then said, "Well, the only way I know how to answer that is to tell you that my father was an alcoholic. I didn't know him. And the greatest influence in my life was my mother. And Jesus is more real to me than my mother."

When he said that, I almost fell off the sofa onto the floor. When I probed further, I found a real genuineness there. It wasn't as if he'd been schooled theologically; it was just a reality for him. Over the ensuing weeks and months, I was able to see the truth of what he had said, and he proved to have a teachable spirit when it came to spiritual matters.

Michael Deaver became a Christian before he died, and for the last few years of his life we were good friends. We prayed and talked together about our concerns for our nation. He told me once that if it hadn't been for resistance from establishment Republicans like himself—I often referred to them as the Republican Guard—there was no limit to what the Reagan Administration could have accomplished.

When I told Mike that he might have actually kept Reagan from hearing some of the spiritual wisdom and insights that would have been incredibly meaningful, he replied, "Reagan, in my opinion, was the greatest president of the twentieth century. Had it not been for people like me, keeping godly people away from him and wise people away from him, I think he could have been perhaps the greatest president in American history." He also told me about the complexities of what happens to a president who is cut off from the very wisdom he needs; how difficult it is for people in the White House and Oval Office to really hear wise counsel, especially of a spiritual nature. This clearly confirms the legitimate concern that many Americans have about the misguided political control frequently referred to as "the Establishment," or what Senator Ted Cruz has referred to as "the Washington Cartel." It's a serious problem, and Americans are rightly fed up with it, just as they are fed up with political correctness and bias in the media. This foolishness must end.

The National Affairs Briefing

On August 20, 1980, more than seventeen thousand Christian conservatives gathered in Dallas for the National Affairs Briefing. Ronald Reagan immediately won over the crowd with his opening remarks, which included a line I had suggested he use.

"I know this is a nonpartisan gathering," Reagan said, "and so I know that you can't endorse *me*. But I only brought that up because I want you to know that *I* endorse *you* and what you're doing."[2]

Reagan spoke after I had given some introductory remarks about the need for people of principle to stand up for godly values. What I said then, and what I still believe, is this:

> How can you expect any politician or any political candidate to stand for principle if the people who believe in principle don't even vote and stand behind them? We're the guilty ones. If there is darkness in the land, it is because of a scarcity of light. Jesus said, "Put the light on the lampstand, not under the bushel". . . .
> If you think our solution is *political*, you too have been deceived. *Don't you commit yourself to some political party or politician. You commit yourself to the principles of God, and you demand those parties and politicians align themselves with the eternal value in [the Bible]. And America will be forever the greatest nation on this earth.*[3]

Just because we answer to a higher calling, a higher standard of truth and righteousness, doesn't mean we're to be uninvolved in the life of our nation. Far from it. It doesn't mean we don't vote. It doesn't mean we don't stand up for what is pure and right and honorable. It doesn't mean we don't try to persuade our legislators to pass God-honoring laws. And it doesn't mean we don't work to keep our government within its constitutional boundaries—as a *protector* (of life and liberty) and not a *provider* of what people don't want to take responsibility for themselves.

> Just because we answer to a higher calling, a higher standard of truth and righteousness, doesn't mean we're to be uninvolved in the life of our nation.

Some in recent years have accused religious conservatives of elevating Ronald Reagan to the level of sainthood, but I couldn't disagree more. If you read or listen to his speech from the 1980 National Affairs Briefing, it's clear that his words still apply every bit as much—and maybe more so—today:

> You and I are meeting at a time when traditional Judeo-Christian values, based on the moral teachings of religion, are undergoing what is perhaps their most serious challenge in our nation's history. Nowhere is the challenge to traditional values more pronounced, or more dangerous, than in the area of public policy debate. So it's fitting that the topic of our meeting should be national affairs. For it is precisely in the affairs of our nation where the challenge to those values is the greatest.
>
> In recent years, we've seen a new and cynical attack on the part of those who would seek to remove from our public policy debate the voice of traditional morality. This tactic seeks not only to discredit traditional moral teachings, but also to exclude them from public debate by intimidation and name-calling as we were so eloquently told just a short time ago.
>
> We have all heard it charged that whenever those with traditional religious values seek to contribute to public policy, they're attempting to impose their views on others. We're told that any

public policy approach incorporating traditional values is out of bounds. This is a matter that transcends partisan politics and demands the attention of every American, regardless of party.

If we have come to a time in the United States when the attempt to see traditional moral values reflected in public policy leaves one open to irresponsible charges, then the structure of our free society is under attack, and the foundation of our freedom is threatened. Under the pretense of separation of church and state, religious beliefs cannot be advocated in many of our public institutions. But atheism can. . . .

When I hear the First Amendment used as a reason to keep traditional moral values away from policy making, I'm shocked. The First Amendment was written not to protect the people and their laws from religious values, but to protect those values from government tyranny. This is what Madison meant when he drafted the Constitution and that precious First Amendment. This is what the state legislatures meant when they ratified it. And this is what a long line of Supreme Court decisions have meant. But over the last two or three decades, the federal government seems to have forgotten both that old time religion and that old time Constitution.[4]

I recently spoke to Jerry Naylor, who was part of Reagan's inner circle back in 1980, to ask him what he remembered about the National Affairs Briefing. He described the feeling of that meeting as "electric," and said that the energy of God's Spirit was all over the place. He also confirmed that most of Reagan's closest advisers had told him not to attend the briefing, but Reagan had pushed back against "the typical establishment advice" and said, "I'm going, and I'm going to listen to James preach."

"After that," Jerry said, "I saw a totally changed Ronald Reagan. It was like he was supercharged with a spiritual energy that was obvious to me." After that gathering in Dallas, everything shifted, and the momentum of support for Reagan began a rapid ascension to his winning the presidency—and then the second time winning every state but one. When I mentioned to Jerry Naylor that Nancy Reagan had told me the next day that she had never seen her husband so excited, he said, "That is exactly the case. Something wonderful happened there."[5]

I'm convinced that Reagan's run for the White House took off because the church *came together* for freedom's sake. People prayed and stood together in unity, and something great happened.

The Shields of the Earth

General Daniel Graham was also at the National Affairs Briefing, and he asked me if I would speak to Ronald Reagan about the impending threat of Soviet missile technology.

"Reagan and I knew each other in California," Graham said, "but he doesn't know what I know, and so far I haven't been able to tell him. Since you've gotten to know him and have developed a relationship, would you tell him that I know how we can build a shield?"

Before the briefing, Reagan and I met, along with former Texas governor John Connolly, and I opened my Bible on the table in front of us and read Psalm 47:9: "The shields of the earth belong to God."

I said, "Sir, do you know what a laser is?" Remember, this was 1980, just three years after the first fiber optic communications system was installed in Chicago, and before compact discs were even introduced, so widespread knowledge of laser technology was still in the early stages.[6]

"No, not exactly," Reagan said.

"It's amplified light. What do you think the light of the world is?"

"Jesus."

"Well," I said, "we need to amplify the light, for freedom's sake."

Reagan nodded, and I said, "But let me share with you what amplified light can do."

147

General Graham was standing somewhere behind us, but I didn't know whether Reagan had seen him in the room. I said, "General Daniel Graham is here, and he wants to share something important with you."

General Graham then sat down and told Reagan what lasers could do to take down missiles. Right there, with the Bible still open on the table to the "shields of the earth belong to God," what the media later pooh-poohed and mocked as "Star Wars" was born. General Graham became head of the Strategic Defense Initiative for the next eight years to develop this protection system, but SDI was eventually abandoned because of the complexities and challenges it presented, tensions between the doves and hawks in Congress, and the collapse of the Soviet Union. And it's not something that has come back to the table. But it was at the National Affairs Briefing in 1980 that the idea first came to Ronald Reagan's attention.

The significance of all this is that two of the greatest Christian leaders of our day, Billy Graham and Bill Bright, heard the same thing from God, at different times, and unbeknown to each other; and they shared the information with some people they trusted, and together we committed the matter to prayer.

I believe that prayer meeting changed the course of history and that God put into place the leader that our nation—and the world—needed to preserve our freedom when a former Hollywood actor was elected president and a good Christian man with a wonderful smile and a kind heart was voted out of the highest office in the land.

Whether anyone wants to believe it, Ronald Reagan *had* to be in leadership at that time. So did Margaret Thatcher. And Pope John Paul. And Lech Walesa. We don't know exactly how all those players arrived in their unique positions of influence at just the right time, but I believe it was supernaturally, miraculously orchestrated by God. I do know that a whole lot of praying was going on among a lot of people whose names nobody knew, or will ever know, and God answered their cries, because God answers prayer.

I also know that when I stood at the Berlin Wall as it was being torn down in 1990 and went from person to person asking, "What brought this wall down?" everyone—including common bystanders, tourists, and many soldiers—answered by saying, "It was prayed down!" President Reagan confirmed that belief during a conversation he and I had. It was an undeniable miracle in so many ways. We stand in need of another such miracle today.

Thirty-seven years after the beginning of the Reagan Revolution, America is again at a crossroads. And the church once again has the opportunity to bind up the wounds of a divided nation. That's what God would have us do, but we must begin by binding up the wounds of a divided church.

What the Bible Says about
LIVING AMAZED

The chief priests and the teachers of the law heard this and began looking for a way to kill him, for they feared him, because the whole crowd was amazed at his teaching.

Mark 11:18 NIV

Jesus said to them, "Render to Caesar the things that are Caesar's, and to God the things that are God's." And they were amazed at Him.

Mark 12:17

They were fearful and amazed, saying to one another, "Who then is this, that He commands even the winds and the water, and they obey Him?"

Luke 8:25

10

God's Amazing Hand on His Church

> Do not be amazed that I said to you, "You must be born again." The wind blows where it wishes and you hear the sound of it, but do not know where it comes from and where it is going; so is everyone who is born of the Spirit.
>
> John 3:7–8

As I write this chapter, our nation is in the midst of the 2016 presidential campaign—a campaign marked by fractious incivility unlike anything I have seen in my lifetime and perhaps unlike any political campaign in the history of the United States. If the contentious primaries and general election campaign show us nothing else, they reveal the dangerous fault lines in our society—the deep divisions not just between right and left, but at the very *core* of both major political parties. Regardless of the outcome of the election (which will be known by the time this book is published), the stage has been set. We will either come together as a people with renewed unity and a revitalized purpose, or our nation will descend into chaos.

The spotlight now shifts to illuminate how the church will respond. Will we be unable to hear what the Holy Spirit is saying because we're not spiritual, because we're too busy saying "I'm of this" or "I am of that," because we're more focused on what divides us than on what unites us—namely our crucified, risen Lord and Savior. Or will we be able to say that, first and foremost, we are ambassadors for Christ, we are salt and light, we are witnesses to truth and conduits of God's unwavering love.

That is where the choice lies right now. It's in the hands of the church. If the church is the body of Christ on earth, and the government is on Christ's shoulders, then we are His shoulders, just as we are His body. That doesn't mean we're trying to establish a theocracy, as some have suggested. It also doesn't mean we're trying to impose our will. We reveal the Savior—who is Himself the way, the truth, and the life.[1] Period. And the Spirit of God will establish His purpose.

When *the* way, *the* truth, and *the* life is revealed, it is undeniable—you can't hide it, and you can't hide from it. Light cannot be covered by darkness. By its very nature, light chases away darkness. In spiritual terms, the light can be covered only when it *allows* itself to be covered. And Jesus told us not to do that.[2] That's in part the vision that Ronald Reagan called us to when he referred to America as a "shining city upon a hill" in his farewell speech to the nation in 1988.[3] Reagan attributed the phrase to John Winthrop, the first governor of the Massachusetts Bay Colony, which serves to underscore and illustrate how deeply ingrained biblical truths and principles were in the founding and flourishing of our nation.

> When the way, the truth, and the life is revealed, it is undeniable—you can't hide it, and you can't hide from it.

With the stage set for chaos, the only calming influence with any credibility is the church. If America doesn't *blow up*, it will be because the church *stood up*. I'm talking about the true church—not as kingmakers or as a political power base, but as channels of God's love and conduits of true, godly wisdom and the transforming power of the Holy Spirit. Nothing short of an amazing, supernatural move of God will get this country back on track.

If the church won't stand up, our nation will not get better. But if we—and our leaders—will hear and respond to the truth, I believe we will recover quickly, just as the Israelites quickly rebuilt the walls of Jerusalem in Nehemiah's day.[4] We will see a rapid turnaround and a swift recovery. Our fundamental need to live amazed has never been more urgent or more real.

Binding Up Our Wounds

When Abraham Lincoln delivered his Second Inaugural Address on March 4, 1865, he spoke to a divided nation. But in his comparison of sides in the conflict, he might just as easily have been writing to the divided church of our day: "Both read the same Bible and pray to the same God, and each invokes His aid against the other."[5]

In the same vein, Lincoln's analysis and prescription are equally apt:

> The prayers of both could not be answered. That of neither has been answered fully. The Almighty has His own purposes. "Woe unto the world because of offenses; for it must needs be that offenses come, but woe to that man by whom the offense cometh". . . .
>
> With malice toward none, with charity for all, with firmness in the right as God gives us to see the right, let us strive on to finish the work we are in, to bind up the nation's wounds, to care for him who shall have borne the battle and for his widow and his orphan, to do all which may achieve and cherish a just and lasting peace among ourselves and with [everyone].[6]

The church of Jesus Christ today is largely controlled by a spirit of fear and intimidation. It's tragic. "But perfect love casts out fear."[7] And we're not to walk in intimidation, for "we are more than conquerors."[8] What does that mean? "Where the Spirit of the Lord is, there is freedom," and we're to walk in that freedom.[9]

Freedom doesn't mean that anything goes. Freedom means that we unreservedly submit ourselves to the power and wisdom of the Holy Spirit, we test the spirits together to see whether something is from God,[10] and then we move forward with boldness, grace, and mercy, exhibiting in every aspect of our lives the fruit of the Spirit, which should be evident in our lives if we are truly walking in the Spirit. There is no law against the fruit of the Spirit. It is always good, pure, and right.

If we are to bind up the wounds of the church and bind up the wounds of the nation, we must realize—and acknowledge—that God works through *all* parts of His body. And we must stop trying to limit His hand with our differences. There's too much calling of this or that prophetic or anointed. People are always trying to identify—or steadfastly denying—the latest moves of God when the simple fact is that God is everywhere, working through His people to accomplish His purpose in the world.

Moving beyond the Lines We've Drawn

We don't have to put labels on everything we do. In fact, those labels are often what have kept us apart and held us in bondage. When I spoke to the board at Oral Roberts University one time, I urged them to take ORU *beyond* Pentecostal boundaries; to move out and do what God wants to do. It's the same conversation I had with Jerry Falwell when I suggested that he take the word *Baptist* off the college that is now known as Liberty University (which Jerry founded). I wanted his work to have an impact on the entire church, not just part of it.

There was a time when Jerry was quite unhappy with me. He didn't like me hanging out with Pentecostals and charismatics.

But before long, he was grabbing me in one of his classic bear hugs and our friendship remained strong. In recent years, Liberty University has been stretched beyond its Baptist roots to become more inclusive, and I think that people from diverse groups are feeling increasingly comfortable there. And God has blessed Liberty because of that. That doesn't mean everything the school does is perfect, but it's taking strides in the direction of God's leading.

We evangelicals need to unify around the gospel of Jesus Christ and stop treating people who are different from us like something we don't like. We have to get the barriers down, and people have to learn to love one another. It's like the dialogue we have with many in the Catholic Church. It pleases God when we sit down together and honor the Lord. And we have to learn to do that.

God is pleased when we show up, ready and willing to allow Him to work through us as conduits of His grace. We must remain as yielded clay in the hands of the Potter, surrendered to His purpose, His vision, His plan. That way, *God* gets *all* the glory. We must resist the temptation to take upon ourselves that which the Father has reserved for Himself.

Likewise, we must resist the temptation to *judge* that which God has said *He* will judge. When Christ returns, He will separate the sheep from the goats; He will establish the judgment seat, before which all must give an account of their lives. Our job is to "fervently love one another from the heart."[11] And while there is still time, we are to convey the love of God to those who need to hear it, who need to feel it, who need to be enveloped by it.

Are we to be discerning? Absolutely. But let's not tear down what God has built up, and let's not make judgments about the motives of brothers and sisters in Christ who are pursuing God's purpose and plan in their lives with as much wisdom, understanding, and integrity as they can muster—just like you are. If you want to weigh in with your opinion about someone else's ministry or someone else's life, weigh in with God. The effective, fervent prayers of the righteous availeth much.[12]

We're also to leave to the Holy Spirit that which is His responsibility. Jesus said that He would send the Spirit to "convict the world concerning sin and righteousness and judgment."[13] Our role is to "build each other up in . . . holy faith, pray in the power of the Holy Spirit, and await the mercy of our Lord Jesus Christ, who will bring . . . eternal life."[14] We are to "show mercy to those whose faith is wavering; rescue others by snatching them from the flames of judgment; [and] show mercy to still others . . . with great caution, hating the sins that contaminate their lives."[15]

In recent years, God has given me the joy of seeing many barriers come down. And I'm still seeing it. If you knew the people I sat with at a recent pastors conference, you would be amazed. These are people you would not expect to find in the same place together. And yet there they were—and they were loving one another. As I see what love and understanding can accomplish, I look forward to the day when we all will stand openly together. I believe that day is coming.

How God Breaks Down Barriers

Even before God "stretched" me, I saw the need for the whole body of Christ to be heard. One of the things I told Paul Crouch at Trinity Broadcasting Network (TBN) is that God could use the network to allow the body of Christ to meet one another. To me, that was a significant message I gave him, and he followed up on it. I was the first non-Pentecostal to go on TBN, and at Paul's request I brought other evangelicals onto the network. I encouraged Jerry Falwell to become part of the network's lineup with his *Old Time Gospel Hour*, as well as Ed Young with *Winning Walk*, and Adrian Rogers with *Love Worth Finding*.

I didn't agree with a lot of what TBN did, but I still saw it as a valuable tool for bringing the church together and opening a dialogue. I agreed with a fellow pastor who once said to me that TBN telethons looked like "spiritual seduction and manipulation." And I never like to hear preachers tell people that if they give a gift to God, or to some ministry, all their bills will be paid, even though they haven't learned how to manage their money.

I wrote an entire book on true prosperity, concerning the joy of giving to *give*, not to *get*; on blessing others to bless, which in itself is blessing enough. We certainly reap what we sow, but it's a big mistake to define "blessings" as monetary, because no reliable monetary or material standard of measure exists.

When we engage with people whose views don't align perfectly with ours and treat them with love and respect, we open up avenues of communication through which we can speak the truth in love. But if they never know that we love them, then they will never be able to hear us.

Over the years, I've learned that one way to lay a good foundation for developing relationships with preachers from a wide variety of backgrounds is to express my appreciation for the giftedness of the preacher—whether it's someone such as Jack Graham, Matt Chandler, Tony Evans, T. D. Jakes, Joseph Prince, Joyce Meyer, Joel Osteen, Michael Brown, John MacArthur, Jack Hayford, Erwin Lutzer, David Jeremiah, or somebody in the Catholic community whose preaching magnifies the Lord. It also helps to go back and look at the church fathers—who were, in fact, Catholic—and see what they have contributed to the life of the body.

I preached one time at Regent University, a charismatic university founded by Pat Robertson, along with a Billy Graham associate, Jack Hayford, and Father Raniero Cantalamessa, who has served as "Preacher to the Papal Household" since 1980.[16] Cantalamessa preached biblical truth taught by Martin Luther, affirming the theological principle of salvation by grace through faith. By the end of the sermon, the students were cheering. Who would've thought that would ever happen? All of us—Baptists, Pentecostals, and Catholics—were preaching Christ. What's unhealthy about that?

It's time for the body of Christ to come together in the unity that Jesus prayed for in John 17. It's time for the pancreas to give proper recognition to the lungs and for the eyes to give proper regard to the ears, the hands, and the feet. All members of the body must recognize that all members of the body have a place and a purpose. And we don't need the spleen to rupture every time something happens that stretches our comfort zone or that we can't explain.

> It's time for the body of Christ to come together in the unity that Jesus prayed for in John 17.

Iron Sharpening Iron

Misapplication of Proverbs 27:17—"Iron sharpens iron, so one man sharpens another"—has led to some nasty stab wounds over the years. If we Christians are going to pull out the swords, we need to stop criticizing one another and start honing and sharpening one another. It would please the Lord no end if we in the church would stop squaring off and instead would come alongside one another and do the work of iron sharpening iron.

We focus too much on ourselves and our own perspectives. Rick Warren hit the nail on the head in the opening sentence of *The Purpose Driven Life*: "It's not about you."[17] It's all about God—and other people. We're called to love God with all our hearts, and to love our neighbor as ourselves. We want the best for them, just as we want it for ourselves.

There's nothing wrong with wanting the best for ourselves and our families, but what do we do to get it? Do we say something manipulative or disingenuous, rather than speaking the truth?

Do we think only about ourselves? Are we too self-absorbed to even understand what it means to look at others?

Yes, we need to get the truth out. But when others try to communicate truth and don't say it exactly correctly (or how we would say it), it's not our divine assignment to straighten them out by damaging them in any way we can. That's the way of the political arena; that's the way of many academic circles; and, tragically, too often it's the way of the church and those who speak on behalf of the church. Rather than correct and heal, we have a tendency to attack and damage. It's brutal.

When a well-known preacher said that fellow pastor Steven Furtick, whom he had never met, was unqualified, he struck an unintended chord. What was offered as a dismissive judgment became an inspiration. In 2016, Furtick wrote a book titled *(Un)Qualified*, because, he said, "I've *always* felt that way. I feel that way as a pastor. I feel that way as a husband. I feel that way as a dad. Who *doesn't* feel that way?" In the end, he said, the criticism "set me free from the need to perform, knowing that God produces results in my life."[18]

Has Steven Furtick been exposed to all the iron-sharpening relationships, all the honing and shaping that need to happen in his life? Maybe not. But we *all* need that. If we believe that someone we know is in need of correction, we have an obligation to speak the truth in love. But first we must love. Iron sharpening iron is meant to happen in relationship.

There is no shortage of people in our churches, neighborhoods, and communities who feel unqualified, unworthy, and ineffective. Many, if not most, feel overlooked as well. And that's how they live. My journeys throughout the world have shown me, and reminded me, how overlooked and forgotten most people feel. Even here in America, in the midst of our material abundance, people feel overlooked and unworthy. I believe God would be thrilled to see mature and established believers take younger, less mature believers under their wings in mentoring relationships. How many qualified people are sitting in the pews every week surrounded by weaker vessels who need to be shown how important they are to God—and how important God's mission and role for them is? If we could mobilize this untapped resource in the body of Christ, I think we would accomplish an amazing goal by linking mentors with protégés in the spirit of Timothy, Titus, and Paul.

We also must be willing to accept correction from others, even if it seems unloving. I've told many visible church leaders not to scrap the things people write about them that scrutinize or even criticize them. "Take it to the Lord; don't just automatically discount what people say. See if there's something you need to hear from God. Examine your own direction." The fact that we can have these conversations builds the kind of practice that I believe needs to happen with all Christians, where we talk about important things and seek to sharpen one another's faith.

When Kenneth Taylor first published *The Living Bible*, it became a bestseller, but critics jumped all over him. He responded graciously, saying it was a paraphrase of the Bible, like a sermon. From the seeds of *The Living Bible*, Tyndale House Publishers developed the New Living Translation, which has become one of the top-selling translations of the Bible on the market. When I met with Ken Taylor, I thanked him for his diligence and desire to make the Word of God easier to understand. I wanted to be an encouragement to him.

When we speak the truth in love, instead of criticizing and condemning, we open doors of dialogue and gain access to opportunities to offer constructive correction—if and when it's needed. I preach to Baptists, Catholics, and charismatics. I'll preach to anyone. And I haven't changed any of my theological positions. But I hope that I exhibit grace toward those I might disagree with. I think some preachers are as wrong as they can be about their dispensations, end-time prophecies, and other theological positions, but I'm not going to be unkind, unloving, or disrespectful to them. Because *I* might be wrong. After all, we all have much to learn.

You'll find correction to the Vatican and the pope every week on our website, The Stream (https://stream.org), written by concerned, in-love-with-Jesus Catholics. And the Catholic Church isn't coming back at us, because everything we say is said in love. We're speaking corrective words to others in the body of Christ as well, and we're not getting pushback, because it's hard to push back in the face of consistent love. Love doesn't fail. Somewhere it gets through. And it has to get through, because the world is so full of hate today.

On *LIFE Today*, Betty and I have people from every vein of the Christian community, many who would never be in a room together otherwise, appear together as guests because we are seeking to serve and love them. We want to help them become all that God wants them to be—in life and in ministry.

God spoke to me at the height of my crusade ministry and told me I would be far more effective if I adopted a servant mentality and simply tried to convey the love of God to people. And I have seen a greater impact since I made the decision to sit down on a sofa in a television studio with my wife than I saw while preaching to big crowds. Though I had decades of successful ministry as a crusade evangelist, winning people to Christ, when I began helping *others* win people to Christ, I saw more people won to Christ than ever before. And Jesus is clearly at the center, not some great superstar evangelist or celebrity preacher. As important as the preaching is, we can't make preachers, or teachers, the objects of our devotion.

Don't Despise Small Beginnings

In our iron-sharpening efforts, we would be wise not to despise small beginnings. We have no idea how God may choose to ignite a bonfire from a flickering flame.

When my pastor, Robert Morris, was a teenager and dating Debbie, the young woman who would become his wife, the two of them came to meet with me and I had an opportunity to spend some time with them and speak into their lives. Later, Robert joined my ministry team for a while, and I was able to share with him about the stretching experience that had allowed me to walk in greater freedom.

When Robert had a powerful encounter of his own with the Holy Spirit, he experienced a lot of scrutiny and pressure because he was a student at the Criswell Center for Biblical Studies at the time. Though he was criticized and misunderstood, he continued to respond in love.

When Robert and Debbie were thinking about starting a church, I suggested they look at Southlake, a community just north of Dallas-Fort Worth, and that's where they ended up. What God has done through Robert as pastor of Gateway Church has been nothing short of amazing. How else can you explain a congregation that has grown from thirty people to thirty-six thousand in less than twenty years—and in an upscale community where people don't have time for God? How else can you explain a church that received $20 million in offerings last year *over and above* the $120 million budget for the year and is giving away more money to missions than most churches could even dream of? It's mind-boggling.

And now it looks as if Robert's son Josh is following in his footsteps and may have an even greater anointing to preach than his father does. The only way to account for all this is to acknowledge the amazing hand of God at work.

But here's the point I don't want you to miss: God can do amazing work through any yielded life—for *His* glory and *His* purpose. Will it look exactly like what He has done with me or with Robert Morris? Most likely not. But it will be no less amazing. In fact, it might be even more amazing. When I look at what God has done in my life, and in Robert Morris's life, and in the lives of so many others I have seen firsthand, I know without a doubt that there is no limit to what God can do with any life that is surrendered to Him.

The Charcoal Fire

Not only must we come alongside one another in the work God has for us, but we must also stay together. Think of a charcoal fire and how important it is for the coals to be piled together to make a strong-burning fire. Coals that roll off the edge lose their fire or burn out. As believers did at Pentecost when they assembled together and waited for God, we too must preserve the unity of the Spirit in the bond of peace before we look to God to light the fire.

Far too often, the church isn't yielded to the Holy Spirit, who enables us to live amazed, but instead is controlled by a typical humdrum spirit of the world, a spirit of religion, a spirit of defeat, or maybe even a spirit of bondage. This tendency to settle for only what we can understand and manage must be addressed supernaturally, or else it will prevail. We live in a "religious" world, with religious-minded people. We need to take people to the truth, finding and revealing the hidden treasures of God.

We need to be around people who are being carried by the Spirit of amazement. I'm not talking about Pentecostalism; I'm talking about the ongoing biblical reality of power and infilling that first came on the Day of Pentecost.

The New Testament is a book of amazement. The Old Testament is a book of amazement. Just think about what God has been able to accomplish through people who were flawed, who failed, who fell apart, and yet who were able to fulfill their part of God's life-changing, world-altering, history-making purpose and plan because their lives were yielded to the One who binds up the brokenhearted, sets the captives free, and brings good news to the afflicted. That's what it means to live amazed in the presence of God. That's what it means to walk in the power and life that have been offered to us.

We need that encouragement. We need to bless others. We need to bear one another's burdens, brighten every day, comfort every sorrow, and shoulder every load. We need to affirm the potential of *every* life—no matter what. There are no small, unimportant parts, no insignificant members of the body of Christ.

When I look back over my life, I see times when God really carried me— and He did it through the work and ministry of other Christians, other coals on the fire. But when I became so caught up in the work that I neglected the importance of prayer and meaningful fellowship, I tumbled off the fire and began to burn out on my own. And that can happen at any time. As a fire gets hot, the coals can shift and one or more pieces can fall away. So we must be diligent about staying connected—and helping others stay connected.

> When I look back over my life, I see times when God really carried me—and He did it through the work and ministry of other Christians, other coals on the fire.

When I read John 17 and the prayer Jesus prayed for unity—the thing he emphasized most at the end of His earthly life—I feel refocused. I feel the heat of the fire, burning with the Spirit of God.

I do not ask on behalf of these alone, but for those also who believe in Me through their word; that they may all be one; even as You, Father, are in Me and I in You, that they also may be in Us, so that the world may believe that You sent Me.[19]

I want to see Jesus's prayer answered—we've only seen glimpses of it so far. I want to see it come to fruition.

Stop Comparing Yourself

When I look at Robert Morris and many others and see how they have surpassed me in so many ways in the impact they're having, one of my greatest challenges is not to compare myself and feel that somehow I'm not qualified anymore.

The Christian life is a relay race—how else will our faith be passed along?—except we don't stop running the race that God has laid out for us when we hand off the baton to succeeding generations. Instead, we press on, and God continues to amaze us in every season of life.

Let's not waste time comparing our gifts with others. Let's keep surrendering those gifts back to God and see what He wants to do with them. The day of the somebodies is over—if there ever was such a day. God wants to work through everybody who will yield their life to Him and surrender themselves to His gifting, wisdom, plan, and direction.

God has shown me lately that we don't have time to waste sowing seed on unfertile soil, when there are fields "white for harvest." Neither do we have time to stand around lamenting or pointing fingers at the unfertile soil. If we want to invest our time there, let's invest it as intercessors, praying for the plow of the Holy Spirit to break up the hard ground and prepare it for planting. But let's not stand in the public square, railing on about the drought or the hardness of the soil. Let's get busy bringing in the sheaves.

That isn't to say we're not to be involved in the public square. Far from it. But let's be about the Master's business, not our own.

Testing Your Faith

As a final word for this chapter, I'm drawn to the epistle written by my namesake, James, which offers a host of practical wisdom for living amazed in the body of Christ:

- Live joyfully, knowing that testing produces endurance (1:2–4).
- Ask God for wisdom (1:5).
- Ask in faith, without doubting (1:6).
- Persevere under trial (1:12).
- Avoid deception (1:16).
- Be quick to hear, slow to speak, and slow to anger (1:19).
- Put aside all wickedness (1:21).
- Do the word, don't just listen to it (1:22).
- Bridle your tongue (1:26).
- Don't play favorites (2:1–4).
- Honor the poor (2:6).
- Keep the law of liberty (2:8–13).
- Show your faith by your works (2:14–26).
- Guard your tongue (3:1–12).
- Avoid earthly wisdom. Embrace the "wisdom from above" (3:13–18).
- Check your motives; don't quarrel (4:1–3).
- Don't be a friend of the world and an enemy of God (4:4).
- Submit to God. Resist the devil (4:7).
- Draw near to God; cleanse your hands, purify your hearts (4:8).
- Humble yourself in God's presence (4:10).
- Do not speak against a brother (4:11).
- Your life is a vapor—don't be arrogant and presumptuous (4:13–16).
- Do the right thing (4:17).
- Mourn injustice and repent (5:1–6).
- Be patient (5:7).
- Strengthen your heart (5:8).

- Don't complain about others (5:9).
- Endure (5:10–11).
- Don't swear an oath (5:12).
- Sing praises (5:13).
- Pray for the sick and the suffering, anointing them with oil (5:14).
- Confess your sins to one another. Pray for healing for one another (5:16).
- Turn those who stray back to the truth (5:19).
- Save souls (5:20).

What the Bible Says about
LIVING AMAZED

All those hearing [Saul] continued to be amazed, and were saying, "Is this not he who in Jerusalem destroyed those who called on this name . . . ?"

Acts 9:21

All the circumcised believers who came with Peter were amazed, because the gift of the Holy Spirit had been poured out on the Gentiles also.

Acts 10:45

Peter continued knocking; and when they had opened the door, they saw him and were amazed.

Acts 12:16

11

A Life Filled with Amazing Encounters

When Peter saw this, he replied to the people, "Men of Israel, why are you amazed at this, or why do you gaze at us, as if by our own power or piety we had made him walk?"

Acts 3:12

EVER SINCE I'VE LEARNED how to live amazed, God has never stopped amazing me. Everywhere I go, He shows me new facets of His character, new expressions of His love, and new examples of His life-changing power.

Voice of an Angel

After I was set free, I began to preach fearlessly in all kinds of settings. Many of my Southern Baptist brethren were unhappy with me, or critical, but I never hit back. I just kept loving them. I knew my theology hadn't changed. I had simply been released into a more complete understanding and expression of the work God was doing throughout the Old and New Testaments—and that He continues to do to this day. If I had been afraid of what the Baptists might say, I wouldn't have gone to Jack Hayford's church to preach, I wouldn't have visited Oral Roberts, and I wouldn't have been at a charismatic Maranatha Ministries conference, where I witnessed one of the most amazing things I've ever seen.

I was sitting in the front row as a young man came out onto the platform and prepared to sing. Somebody next to me leaned over and said, "You're going to like this."

When the musician strummed his guitar and started singing in Spanish a song called "Tengo Vida Nueva" ("I Have New Life"), I gasped.

"That's not the voice of a man," I said out loud, "that's the voice of an angel." He was unbelievable.

After the service, I met the singer, James Thomas, and he told me an even more incredible story of how he had come to sing that particular song, which had become extremely popular in Latin America.

"My wife and I were in a little mission church in South America," he said. "At the time, the only Spanish words I knew were *burrito*, *taco*, and *enchilada*. When we got up in front of the church, a visiting preacher prayed for us to receive the gift of Spanish. And in one smooth stroke, Jamie and I both began to speak perfect Spanish. We had a complete vocabulary, in the perfect dialect for where we were, and we both knew what we were saying—it was in our *minds* as well as coming out flawlessly through our mouths. It was an exact Acts 2 manifestation."

Not long after that conference, I brought James and Jamie to meet my staff at LIFE Outreach. One of my upper-level staff members is a woman from Spain. When she heard the Thomases speak, she stood up, astounded, and said, "It is not possible to teach someone to do what they are doing. That is perfect Spanish of the highest level. You can't teach that."

That, my friend, is living amazed.

Carrying the Cross

During a televised meeting of several thousand people one year in Anaheim, California, I was under conviction that I really didn't understand much about ministry, or even how to preach. But that night, the Lord taught me a little bit about how His power can flow through *any* yielded vessel.

In the middle of my sermon, God interrupted me and directed my attention to a man dressed in blue jeans who had come down to the front of the auditorium. He had prostrated himself in front of the platform and was talking to God.

I quickly recognized the man on the floor as Arthur Blessitt, who had become well known for walking across the United States and around the world, carrying a ninety-pound, twelve-foot cross. At the time of this meeting in Anaheim, he had already walked more than twenty-one thousand miles, and today that number is more than forty-one thousand miles. Arthur's life is one long testimony to the reality of living amazed.

I have walked the streets of major cities with Arthur, and I have seen total strangers begin to tremble and drop to their knees within three minutes after Arthur has started talking to them. This has included men in business suits and others who looked like gang members—it didn't matter. Once Arthur started talking to them, it was as if the power of God fell on them from heaven.

I've been with Arthur in restaurants where he has ministered to one of the waiters, and then had several other waiters follow us out to the street to ask Arthur what he had just told the other waiter, because they had seen a supernatural move of God. And I've heard testimonies about the time in 1986 when Arthur and his son Joshua carried the cross into the middle of Johannesburg, South Africa, sat down in Oppenheimer Park, and began to pray. Almost immediately, and for the next seven days, people came up to Arthur to pray and be prayed for—and hundreds of people were saved, and others were healed of various disabilities. Some of these people were ones Arthur prayed for, but others were healed just by walking by, and later came up to Arthur to tell him what had happened.

After an amazing week in Johannesburg, Arthur repeated his fast in Durban and then in Cape Town, and many more people were saved and healed.

When people ask me why God would do such miraculous works through Arthur Blessitt and not through other dedicated and seemingly gifted people, I tell them a few things I've learned through my experiences.

Lesson one is that we don't have to understand everything. The Spirit moves where He will, and we don't always know why He chooses one vessel or another. He's certainly not dealing with perfect people, and that's why we don't exalt individuals. None of us is perfect. Only God is perfect. So we're not gathering around Arthur Blessitt or Billy Graham or James Robison or anyone else. We're gathering around almighty God—and God alone. When we talk about living amazed, the amazing part of that equation is God—what He does with you and me; what we've seen Him do with others. We need to stop being amazed at the paltry gifts of our fellow men and women and turn our eyes to the all-surpassing power, wisdom, and grace of God.

> When we talk about living amazed, the amazing part of that equation is God.

I've also learned the value of relationships, and how vulnerable we are if we become isolated from the body of Christ. It is only in close, committed fellowship with other mature believers that we are able to discern and assess what God is doing in our lives. Alone, we lack perspective and true wisdom, and we become prone to discouragement, deception, and being drawn away.

Finally, I've learned that God's blessing and anointing don't insulate us from attacks by the enemy—all the temptations, doubts, and distractions he throws at us. We need to put on the full armor of God, and in His strength stand firm against the wiles of the devil.[1]

On the night when we were together in Anaheim, Arthur Blessitt, the same man who had seen God work miracles all over the world, was in need of a miracle of his own. He later told me, "You will never know how much, at that very moment, I needed to be ministered to." We all need Jesus to minister to us in our hearts. He uses other people—the members of His body—to touch us, love us, and heal us.

As I turned my attention to Arthur that night, somehow every burden, every pain, every heartache, every moment of loneliness that had ever passed through his mind and person came onto me, and I felt the weight of it as I began to minister to him. It was a powerful and unifying experience.

This was all being televised nationally on TBN, and the cameras zeroed in on Arthur, who was lying prostrate on the floor. As I began to pray for him, hundreds of people started coming forward, and people were falling on their faces before God all over the auditorium. It was unbelievable.

The next afternoon, Arthur and I returned to the empty auditorium to record some TV interviews for later broadcast. As we were sitting together at the front of the room, near the platform, people began drifting into the building and were listening to our interviews.

At one point, Arthur stopped and asked a few of them where they were from. When they said they were from all over the state of California, Arthur said, "Well, what are you doing here?"

"We just drove in," said one couple, "because last night we were watching on television and the Spirit of the Lord fell here."

"It certainly did," Arthur replied. "What was your experience at home?"

"We fell on the floor of our living room in the presence of God."

Another couple said, "The same thing happened to us, and we just had to come. We couldn't stay away."

Over the next twenty-four hours, the testimonies started coming in from tens of thousands of people who had been lying on the floor at home in front of the television, praying *with* Arthur and *for* Arthur.

May we all find ourselves prostrate in spirit in our hearts. And may we be God's instruments to touch the lives of all the people around us with His love.

Sometime after the Anaheim experience, I asked Arthur to come to Texas and share his journey with a group of Christian leaders who had been through the same stretching experience that I'd been through, and who had all been moved by the effectiveness of Arthur's witnessing.

As we all were visiting, Arthur told us that the company that made the boots he wore wanted to sponsor him. He had decided not to accept the sponsorship, but as we sat there, he took off his boots and socks and showed us his feet. There wasn't a single callus anywhere. His feet were as soft and smooth as a baby's backside. This was twenty-five years into his ministry, and he had already walked more than twenty-eight thousand miles. It was simply a miracle of God. There's no other way to explain it.

"You're the first people I've ever shown my feet to," he said, "but I'm showing you because I can tell that you're all very serious about walking with the Lord."

Arthur Blessitt shared some amazing stories with us that day, but when we saw his bare feet, they bore testimony to everything else he had said. He said, "I am shod with the gospel of peace on my feet."

I know this is extreme stuff, but it's absolutely the truth.

God Opens Up Africa and Third-World Countries

I was in Michigan one time, sharing with a large group of pastors and their wives. Afterward, a young pastor and his wife came to talk to me.

"I got involved with the church secretary," the pastor said, "and we compromised our integrity. But we both repented and broke off the affair. When I told my wife, she said she would stand by me and work through it. And when I told the church, they said they would help us and would work to restore us."

"Really?" I said. It is quite common for churches to cut ties with a pastor who has sinned, leaving no real means of restoration, so I was shocked to hear that this congregation was willing to walk the hard road of forgiveness and reconciliation with their pastor.

A few weeks later, I got a call from the pastor's wife, telling me she had just been fired from the church staff. Already facing the difficult task of reconciling with her husband, she now didn't have a job. The situation was not looking good.

Within a matter of weeks, the church had also fired the pastor and told the family they had to move out of their church-owned housing. So now the congregation that was going to restore the pastor and his wife, as well as the church secretary, had put them out on the street. It broke my heart, and I didn't know what to tell him. At the time, LIFE Outreach didn't have the financial strength we have now, which allows us to care for pastors who need to be restored when nobody else will help them. Oftentimes, members of our staff and staff leadership will take up offerings among themselves to help desperate people get through the hurt and pain of their failures, because their own churches so often will have nothing to do with them, even when there is obvious repentance and brokenness.

Without question, this pastor and his precious wife were broken. But along with their young children they were now on their own.

Many months later—perhaps as much as a year or eighteen months—I was invited to do a nationwide outreach at a convention center in Johannesburg, South Africa. This was when the country was still under apartheid, and I preached against it so strongly that some of the local leaders wondered if I would live long enough to get back to the United States. At the time, South Africa was plagued by tension and uncertainty.

Mangosuthu Buthelezi, the Zulu chief and founder of the Inkatha Freedom Party, had predicted a bloodbath if there was a breakdown of the Codesa agreement in pursuit of a new constitution that would end apartheid. Instead, by the power of God's Word, through businessmen and other church leaders who approached the Zulu leader seeking cooperation and preaching love and forgiveness, hundreds of thousands of lives were spared when Buthelezi demonstrated the same kind of compassion and understanding that Nelson Mandela had shown.

But before that outcome became known, I was in South Africa preaching Jesus amid an atmosphere of tension and uncertainty.

While I was in Johannesburg, the young pastor from Michigan contacted me. He and his family were also in South Africa, at the invitation of a missionary who had heard they'd been driven out of their church. This missionary had offered to take care of them while they got back on their feet.

When I heard the news, I said, "I want to meet that missionary. I want to meet that person in the body of Christ whose love for someone who had failed is so great that he would bring them halfway around the world and take care of them so they could rebuild their lives."

That missionary was a South African named Peter Pretorius. When I met him, he told me how the pastor from Michigan had helped him help the poor. The pastor's church had given offerings to help Peter feed starving people in Africa when many churches wouldn't help.

Peter took me to Soweto, one example of the impoverished areas in South Africa. As we looked at that community of misery, Peter said, "These aren't the really poor people in Africa. I wish I could show you the really poor."

He told me how he had been in Mozambique, where people were dying by the dozens all around him, and he had seen an older man, who was thirsty, leaning up against a tree. "I went to get him some water," Peter said, "but by the time I got back, he was dead. He died while I was off getting him a drink."

Peter ended up staying in Mozambique for more than a week, and all he did during that time was bury people—men, women, and children—who had starved to death. Here was Peter, a tobacco farmer and Formula 1 race car driver, whose wife was part of the upper echelon of South African society—the very people who had been taught not to like the black Africans—and he felt so much compassion for the people of Mozambique that he returned to South Africa, rented a big truck, and asked all his neighbors if they would help him fill it with food so he could save lives. From that small beginning, Peter Pretorius founded Joint Aid Management, an international humanitarian relief organization, and started feeding the starving people of Mozambique. At the time of my visit, he told me, "James, right now I'm able to feed ten thousand children every day."

Betty hadn't gone with me to South Africa for the crusade, but after I returned home, Peter invited us both to come back for a visit, which we later did. He took us into Mozambique, which at the time was embroiled in civil war. We were surrounded by Marxist government troops everywhere we went, and at night while we were trying to sleep in our hotel, they were fighting soldiers from the RENAMO rebel movement down in the streets with AK-47s. It was terrifying.

We traveled into some refugee areas in trucks we had to push-start to get them to run, and when I saw all the kids who were dying while trying to get somewhere safe, it broke my heart and changed my life forever. I told Peter, "Betty and I will move over here and help you."

"Please don't," he said. "Please go home and get us the help and support we need so we can stay here to help these people and not be empty-handed."

We went home, not knowing whom, if anyone, we could get to help. In our typical Baptist circles at the time, if you wanted to call a meeting that no one would attend, you would have a prayer meeting or a missions conference.

I could think of no other way to get money to help them, except to sell our ministry's airplane. The ministry had owned an airplane for more than fifteen years, which had allowed us to keep our tight crusade schedules all over the country, but at this point, with our focus shifting overseas, we no longer needed the plane. Fortunately, we were able to sell it, and that was how we first got money to send to Africa.

Next, I told our leadership that I was going to ask our *LIFE Today* viewers if they would help. We began to show people the need and returned many times to all the hard-hit areas of Africa. I went to Rwanda—straight into the pit of hell—in the middle of the genocide against the Tutsis, when there were dead bodies all around and countless traumatized children. I ended up being the first person to preach at the stadium in Kigali after the killing was brought to a halt. I went into Angola throughout the civil war there, as well as into Ethiopia. With oversight from Peter Pretorius, LIFE Outreach began feeding more than five hundred thousand children a week, building emergency hospital units and care facilities and getting emergency medical supplies into clinics in the bush. With Peter's help, we also built the largest orphanage in Rwanda.

At Franklin Graham's invitation, we also went into Sudan and helped support his efforts there. During that time, his wonderful outreach called Operation Christmas Child was birthed. We knew it was a God-given vision for Samaritan's Purse and that it would be greatly blessed.

To our amazement, when we shared on our television show the opportunities on the mission field, not only did our viewers *want* to help, but they also encouraged us to take on other ventures. For instance, viewers suggested that we drill water wells, because it was so obvious everywhere we went that there was no clean water. We've drilled more than five thousand wells, and the overall number of wells has multiplied many times over as churches and other ministries have joined our efforts. Joel Osteen's father, John, told me before he died, "You and Betty brought the mission fields of the world into our homes. And as missions-minded pastors, we're grateful."

The viewers of *LIFE Today* have learned that they truly live amazed as they give to share love, hope, and help with "even the least of them."[2] They have learned firsthand the blessing of diligently seeking to be an answer to someone's prayer. As Isaiah 58 teaches, when we reach out to the hungry and those in need, we find God answering us quickly. The supporters of LIFE Outreach have told us that supporting our mission and relief efforts in the name of Jesus, and for the glory of God, has given them "joy inexpressible and full of glory," as the apostle Peter said.[3]

A country church in Haw River, North Carolina, with fewer than a hundred members at the time, immediately started contributing to our well-drilling ministry. I recently spoke at that church, which has grown to three thousand people over the past ten years, and they have pictures of missionaries and Betty and me and our well-drilling operations all over the walls of their auditorium. And not too long ago they handed us a check that brought their total donations for well-drilling and other outreaches to more than a million dollars. It's truly amazing.

In addition to churches, we receive donations from individual contributors, couples, and sometimes small businesses. People from all economic levels are willing to help.

When you show people a legitimate need, and an effective way to meet it, they *want* to participate. And I'm convinced they would do that here in America, with the pressing needs of so many right here at home, if we would stop putting all the resources into the hands of the government, which mismanages so many of our tax dollars. We have to stop separating compassion and accountability from the outreach, because there's no effective outreach without compassion, no effective social programs without compassion, and no effective social programs without some sense of accountability and oversight. There must be personal responsibility. We can't keep sending people checks without some accountability for what they do with the money. The government cannot provide sufficient oversight because our government agencies are not connected with the people they serve.

We've seen on the mission field that compassionate assistance with accountability works. It changes lives—both now and for eternity. We've been working in Africa now for twenty-five years, and many of the little children whose lives we saved are now community leaders, schoolteachers and professors, law enforcement personnel, and political leaders. Because they were given adequate necessities for survival when they were younger, such as food and water, they were able to grow up and work and have families of their own.

When we started working with Peter Pretorius to feed people in Mozambique, it was the most impoverished nation in the world. Now the country has moved away from Marxism to become a free economy. The situation is not as stable as it needs to be, but Mozambique has seen a dramatic turnaround nonetheless.

Parking Lots, Nightclubs, and Dairy Queens

In a recent conversation with my former crusade director, T. D. Hall, he brought up the first crusade I ever did in the Dallas-Fort Worth metroplex. W. A. Criswell came to hear me, along with many of the other Southern Baptist leaders who then got behind my ministry.

T. D. said, "I remember you going to all the parking lots, James, and it was the most unbelievable thing." He started reminding me of some of the things that had happened in these places, some of which were dangerous hangouts after dark.

"You would walk into the middle of a crowd and the kids would gather around, and the next thing you know it was like a Holy Spirit–filled meeting right there in the parking lot. It was so amazing what God did."

It *was* amazing, and we saw some miraculous life transformations take place out there.

Kids today have different places where they hang out, but back then it would be a pizza place, a Dairy Queen, or the parking lot at a strip mall. Hundreds of kids would mill around in some of these mall parking lots at night. Some would smoke dope or drink. I would get out there and have a little group surrounding me, and the next thing you knew fifty or a hundred kids would be gathered around, and then two or three hundred. I would just start talking to them, and kids would start repenting and coming to Christ.

Other times I would be driving somewhere and pull into a truck stop where a bunch of truckers would be sitting around a table drinking beer, eating a sandwich, or just chewing the fat. I would walk up, stand at the head of the table, and ask, "Pardon me, but can I tell you something?"

They would look up at me, and I would tell my story real quick—I was conceived when my mother was raped. A doctor wouldn't abort me, so I got to be born, but I grew up without a dad. He was a drunk and wasn't around much. But then Jesus changed my life. He did this and that in my life, and He's wonderful. Then I would say, "I just wanted to tell all you men that I know you're out here working hard, and many of you work tough hours, and I want to believe you're not doing it only so you can go buy a beer. I want to believe you're doing it because you love your wife and your kids. At least I hope you do, because I didn't have a dad—and it's pretty tough for a kid not to have a dad. But I met God, and He's my Father now. And I just wanted to tell all you men that I think you're trying to do what's right. I don't know what's going on in your life, but God sure does love you. And He sure does want to show you how to love your family."

While I was talking, I would see men pushing their beer bottles back on the table, away from themselves. And during these exchanges I never once got yelled or cussed at. I can't explain it, apart from the grace of God and because I was expressing His love to these people.

Sometimes when the team and I would go to get something to eat after a crusade meeting, the only place open where we could get a decent meal would be a nightclub. Many times I would go up onto the stage, walk over to whoever was in charge, and ask, "Can I just say something?" And they would hand me the microphone. Every time!

I would look out at all the people and say, "May I have your attention for a minute?" For whatever reason, they'd look up at me, and I'd say, "I'm just here because I care about you, and I just want to tell you my story." I would give a quick rundown of my life, ending with, "God is great, and I wanted you to know how much He loves you."

Two members of our ministry team who would usually be with me were worship leader Jeanne Rogers and tenor John McKay, who both have remarkable voices.

I would tell the audience at the clubs, "I've got two of the greatest singers in the country sitting out here. One had a leading role in a production of Rodgers and Hammerstein's *Oklahoma!* and the other was the lead singer at several major entertainment venues. I'd love for you to listen to Jeanne Rogers or John McKay sing." And the people would let them sing.

They would start with a hit song, and everyone would start clapping, sometimes giving them a standing ovation. Then sometimes John or Jeanne would say, "Can I sing another song? It's my favorite," and they'd sing a powerful gospel song.

Jeanne would sing about the love of God, while John would often sing about the second coming. And he'd end by saying, "But until then, my heart will go on singing."

Their performances would blow everyone away.

I've lived a wild and crazy life, you might say. When God would move on me, I would immediately respond; and it's still the same way today. I don't get up in front of nightclub audiences anymore, because now a lot of people would know who I am when I stand up. They'd say, "That's the guy on TV, James Robison," and it might take some of the edge off, because, "Yeah, he's just a preacher." But back then no one knew who I was. I was just a guy who cared about them and wanted to tell them about Jesus.

Sometimes when I would tell a stadium crowd about witnessing to people in unique places, they would really take to heart what I said.

I was preaching one time at the high school stadium in Weatherford, Texas, which is a rapidly growing town west of Fort Worth, and when I started talking about how God will use us anywhere—even in parking lots and at Dairy Queens—all of a sudden about ten kids right down in the front row jumped up and started walking out of the stadium.

"Hey, where y'all going?" I asked.

They pointed off toward the end of the stadium and said, "The Dairy Queen's right over there. We're going to get all the kids."

I just laughed and kept on preaching.

With maybe ten minutes left in my message, I looked off to the side and saw about twenty or thirty kids walking into the stadium with the young people who had left to go witnessing. They mingled in with the crowd and sat down. When I gave the invitation, most of these kids came forward together and accepted Christ. Things like that happened *everywhere* I preached.

Downpours and Diversions

One time while I was preaching in Chattanooga, Tennessee, a huge storm was headed straight for the stadium. The clouds gathered on the horizon, and it looked ominous. As the dark clouds drew closer, I said, "Let's just stop and pray. We don't need that storm."

No sooner had I finished praying and looked back up at the sky, when the storm front split in two and traveled right past the stadium on either side. It was like the parting of the Red Sea, and everyone in the stadium saw it happen. Coincidence? Luck? Call it what you want. All I know is that it happened.

On another occasion we were in Decatur, Alabama, at a stadium with seven thousand people. It was springtime, and a huge thunderstorm came rolling in. When it started to rain, the crew came out and covered me with a big umbrella. But it quickly became apparent that the storm was going to be a frog-strangler. Within minutes it was raining so hard that I could hardly see the people in the front rows, let alone anyone farther back. And it just kept raining. I later heard an estimate that it was coming down at two or three inches per hour. But here's the incredible part: *the people didn't leave.* They were bunched up under their umbrellas, getting soaked to the bone, but they stayed and listened to me preach.

When I gave the invitation, hundreds of people left their seats in the stadium and came down to the track, where the water was running over the tops of their shoes, and prayed with me to receive Christ. I have no explanation for that, other than the power of the gospel.

Another memorable moment came in Cleveland, Tennessee, when on the Friday night of the crusade the high school football team was playing. Several people told me that most of the cheerleaders and the marching band had decided to come to the crusade instead of going to the game. I even heard that some of the players hadn't wanted to play in the game, though of course they did. I had to forcefully insist that the cheerleaders and band members leave the crusade meeting and go to the football game. They got there late, but they went. What kind of move of God does it take to make cheerleaders and band members not want to go to a football game at which they are performing? That's crazy. But that's what happened.

I've had a remarkable journey in life, and now that I'm in my seventies, I'm still having one. It's staggering to see what God has done, not just in Bible times, but in our modern times as well.

What the Bible Says about
LIVING AMAZED

Entering the tomb, they saw a young man sitting at the right, wearing a white robe; and they were amazed.

Mark 16:5

The proconsul believed when he saw what had happened, being amazed at the teaching of the Lord.

Acts 13:12

12

God's Amazing Work in the World

They went out quickly and fled from the tomb, for
they trembled and were amazed.

Mark 16:8 NKJV

ONE GOAL of the Christian life that seems to be the most difficult to accomplish and the most assaulted by Satan is spiritual unity among the family of God. We should not only pray for unity, as Jesus prays in John 17, but we should also pray to be an *answer* to what He prayed. Accordingly, I have been bringing Christian leaders together for years and praying for supernatural unity to take hold across the body of Christ.

As part of this effort—which has included getting together with evangelicals, charismatics, and Pentecostals—I began developing relationships with Catholic leaders who are totally in love with Jesus and know Him personally. Many Catholics—as well as many Protestants—have missed the mark or been misdirected theologically at times. But that doesn't mean we can't work together. We could discuss our differences until Christ returns—and some folks seem determined to do just that—but I think we can disagree and still love one another. We can still seek to do things together that are effective in advancing the kingdom of God on earth. And I think that's healthy.

I have a friend who happened to be close to an Argentinian Catholic bishop named Jorge Mario Bergoglio. This man had such a great relationship with Bishop Bergoglio that he prayed for him to experience the fullness of the Holy Spirit—and God gave the bishop an incredible encounter with the power of the Holy Spirit. Bishop Bergoglio has shared this story with as many as fifty thousand people in St. Peter's Square since becoming Pope Francis in 2013. The pope is unapologetic about believing in the power of the Holy Spirit and what the New Testament book of Acts teaches, and he's very bold about it.

Our mutual friend was a missionary we had supported at LIFE Outreach, and Pope Francis was aware of our mission work in Africa, where we have made use of Catholic compounds in various African nations. The Catholics built these compounds to protect the food and goods that are used to care for the poor. We don't allow the governments there to control the food or the things we do in any way, because we've found they cannot be trusted and we don't want our food to end up on the black market. So we have made use of these compounds and have built strong relationships with the Catholics there.

Because Pope Francis cares about the poor and knew about the missionary work we and others were doing in Africa, he asked our mutual friend if he would bring together a group of evangelical leaders to meet with him and pray for unity.

So in June 2014, Betty and I traveled to the Vatican with a small group and met with Pope Francis for almost three hours. As we shared together, I told the pope, "I was christened in the Episcopal Church when I was a boy, but I didn't know the Lord and my heart didn't change. My wife, Betty, was a Sunday school teacher in a Baptist church and a choir member who would often sing solos or duets with her sister. She was also the sweetest girl I had ever known, but even though Betty was baptized, she didn't know the Lord.

"And then we both had a personal encounter with Jesus and were born again. But, sir, I believe I know many Protestants who are members of a church but have never had a real relationship with Christ. They don't know Christ personally. And this breaks my heart because it was true of Betty and me as well. And, sir, I see a lot of Catholics who go through the traditional rituals, but I don't think they know the Lord. I don't believe they know Christ personally. I don't think they've had that spiritual birth."

Pope Francis responded by preaching to those of us gathered there one of the most powerful evangelistic sermons I have ever heard. He emphasized that everyone must be born of the Spirit and have a personal encounter and a personal relationship with Christ. He also acknowledged that many in the church, including some priests, simply do not have that personal relationship with Christ.

When he said that, I was so surprised by his forcefulness that I said, "Sir, I'm an evangelist, and you just delivered a great evangelistic message. Now I don't know if you know what this is, but I think this deserves a high five."

The translator told the pope what I had said and kind of held up his hand to demonstrate what I meant. And in the next moment, Pope Francis gave me the first papal high five in history.

Several Catholic writers noted the significance of the meeting and that no one took issue with the pope about it. On my side, of course, a few complained or asked, "Why were you there with the pope?" Well, we were magnifying Jesus together.

I'm never going to stop seeking to see Christ's prayer for unity answered or to be part of the answer to that prayer.[1] Our nation and our world will never heal without it. We'll also never see a spiritual awakening without it. And if the points in that prayer were important enough for Jesus to pray in His last moments with His disciples, I believe it ought to be important to us as well. So I'm going to continue to build bridges in answer to that prayer.

The Apostle and the Love of God

In 1984, the same year that Robert Duvall won the Academy Award for his performance in *Tender Mercies*, I got a call from one of his associates. He told me that Robert watched me on television, loved to hear me preach, and wanted to meet me.

When I told the caller I was shocked that Robert Duvall would have even noticed my ministry, he said, "Well, Robert is very interested in Christianity, and he believes that preaching is an American art form. He thinks a lot of preachers are phonies, but there are many who are real—and he thinks you're one of the real ones. He just loves your sermons, and he said, 'I just want to meet him—to see if he's real like I think he is.' So would you have time to talk to him?"

I said I'd be happy to.

When Robert and I connected, he said, "People want to know if I'm a Christian. You know, they say, 'Have you been born again?' I don't like to use the terminology, because I see people who say they're Christians, who say they're 'born again,' and they're not anything like Christ. It's terrible the way some church people act and treat each other. It's almost like a comedy. But I've also seen a lot that's real."

He started talking about some ordinary people he'd met— even some who lived in impoverished areas of Appalachia—who had such a love for God that it was remarkable. He mentioned one woman in particular and said, "I have to be honest. I saw Christ in her."

As we continued to talk, he said, "James, you're one of the best preachers I've ever heard. I don't think you're a phony. I'd really like to come to your home and meet your family. Could that be arranged?"

"Betty and I would love to have you over," I said.

When Robert came to our house, we had a tremendous time visiting and getting to know each other. In the course of the conversation, he said, "In one of your crusades that I saw on television, you gave the most powerful illustration of the love of God. Now I need to ask you something. I'm going to do a movie about a preacher. He's got some problems, and his church is full of typical church people, and I want your story to be the climax of my movie about this preacher. I want to show people the love of God."

He was referring to a story I told at a crusade in Memphis in 1980. Here's what I said:

When my son was very small, he used to crawl up in my lap and put his hands up on my face. And he'd say, "Daddy . . . I love you."

I remember when that little fella finally began to walk, he was very heavy—he was a big boy when he was a baby. And I remember the first time I entered my home and those chubby little legs carried him rapidly down that hall with those fat little fists up in the air, saying, "Daddy! Daddy! Daddy! Daddy!" And I grabbed him, and he put those little hands on my face. And I grabbed them, and I looked at the little dimples in each knuckle, and I kissed them, and I turned them over and I kissed them.

And as I held my little boy's hand, and I thought how master-fully God created us, I suddenly saw in that beautiful little hand a horrible nail. And I began to think, *God, I wouldn't let someone come in my house and take my little boy and take him out in my yard and get some old boards and put my little boy on boards and take big old nails and put 'em on his little hands, and while he looked up at me and cried, "Daddy! Daddy!" I wouldn't let them drive those nails through his little hands*! I don't love anyone that much. But *God* does.

When Robert made the movie *The Apostle* in 1997, there's a scene in which his character, the preacher, takes a little baby out of his father's arms at the front of the church, holds him up for the congregation to see, and then tells a version of my story.

> Look at these beautiful, beautiful little hands. Look at 'em. Now imagine a nail piercing the palms of this child's hands. And then picture the nails going into an old board. If you was to take two boards and nail them together, I know I don't have that much love in me, to do this to *my* son, do *you*? I know *I* don't. I don't have that much love *in* me. But God *does*. God *does*. God *does*."[2]

About five months after the movie premiered, we had Robert as a guest on *LIFE Today* and showed video clips of my original telling of the story and Robert's version from the movie. It was a powerful reminder of the depth of love it took for God to allow His Son, who had done no wrong, to give His life so that we might have life everlasting.

"The Greatest" and One Even Greater

When Muhammad Ali died on June 3, 2016, at the age of seventy-four, I thought back to the day when I was privileged and surprised to meet with him privately not long before his retirement from the ring. I was in Southern California for an interview and was riding in a limousine provided by our hosts, along with publicist Duane Ward, founder of Premiere Speakers Bureau, who is one of those people who can open any door and who sees every challenge as an opportunity. We were somewhere between Hollywood and Beverly Hills when the driver pointed to a house we were passing and said, "There's Muhammad Ali's house."

Duane immediately said, "Stop. Stop the car."

When the driver obliged, Duane said, "James, I'm gonna go see if he's home, see if he knows you."

I said, "What? You can't do that. You can't just walk up to somebody's door like that." But Duane was already out of the car and on his way up the walk.

A few minutes later, he came back to the car and I could see somebody standing at the door of the house.

"C'mon, James," Duane said. "Ali's here. He wants to talk to you."

This is crazy, I said to myself, but I got out of the car and walked up to the front door. As I stepped into the entryway, I saw a room off to the side with a prayer rug set out on the floor.

I shook hands with Ali, and before we even sat down to visit, he said emphatically, "I am the most famous person in the world."

His boldness knocked me back, but I responded, "I think you're right."

"*I am* the most *famous* person in the world," Ali said again, with even greater emphasis. "I'm more famous than the president. I'm more famous than the pope. I'm more famous than Billy Graham. *I am* the most *famous* person in the world."

No doubt he was. I've been around a lot of famous people in my life, but being in the same room with Muhammad Ali was clearly something different. I found myself thinking as I stood there in his house, *This has to be a miracle.*

As we talked, Ali told me that some prominent Muslim leaders had approached him about becoming a Muslim evangelist after his boxing career was over.

"They want me to be the Muslim Billy Graham," he said. "And they've offered me a 747 to travel in."

"I hope and pray you won't do that," I said.

The conversation moved away from that discussion, and I began to tell him my life story—about my conversion and how the Holy Spirit took control of my life. How God turned the shiest kid in school into a very bold spokesman. And Ali indicated he had heard of me.

As we continued to visit, he expressed interest in some of the parallels between his own experience and the kinds of places I had lived and the pressures I'd felt. I told him I knew what it felt like to be in the minority—as a minority white. Where I grew up in Austin, only 10 or 15 percent of the population was Caucasian, with the majority being Hispanic and some blacks. I told him about the gang fights, and the fear, and the difficulty of growing up without a dad.

At one point Ali said, "Come in here, let me show you something." He took me into the room where I had seen the prayer rug, got down on the floor, and showed me how he prayed.

"I'm a Muslim," he said, "and I do this several times a day." This was in the early 1980s, before there was much awareness in America about the Muslim faith. So this was all new to me. He told me all the particulars of how he prayed—how often and how long. And it was obvious that he was very dedicated and sincere about what he believed.

After we returned to the living room, I began to tell him about how sincere I was in my relationship to Christ.

"Jesus is the white man's God," Ali said, though he made it clear he had some respect and regard for Jesus as a prophet or a great man—but not in the same class as the prophet Muhammad.

When the conversation had run its course, I was shocked to discover that Duane and I had been there for almost two hours. As we stood up to go, I extended my arm to show Ali what my reach would be if I were a boxer. Though he and I were about the same height, six foot three, I've always had long arms.

"Could you get inside this?" I asked.

With a smile, he put his fist forward, and I could see that his jab would not reach either my chin or my chest, because my arms were so long—thirty-seven inches to the wrist.

"Now what does that do to you?" I asked.

He told me he was so fast it wouldn't matter—and no doubt it wouldn't have. We both stood there and grinned at each other.

All this time, Ali was his usual eloquent self—"float like a butterfly, sting like a bee; nobody in the world can keep up with me"—and he could not have been more gracious to his two drop-in guests.

As we left Ali's house, he surprised me by walking all the way out to the car with us.

"You know," I said, "it would really be great if you were communicating for Jesus."

"Nah."

"But you are the most famous person in the world, and Jesus can change people."

He said he didn't like how Christians were inconsistent and didn't treat one another right. And I couldn't argue because I also had seen it too often. But I kept emphasizing the love of God and the world's love for Ali, including how much I admired and respected him. I asked if I could say a prayer before we left, and he agreed.

Just before I got into the car, Ali looked me straight in the eye and said, "You know, if I'd met someone like you a long time ago, I might love the white man's Jesus."

"Ali, he is *not* the white man's Jesus," I said. "He's *your* Jesus. He's *everybody's* Jesus."

"You know, I think I'm going to come and hear you preach sometime in person."

"Well if you do, I want you to sit on the platform by me. I want everyone to know you're there. And I would like you to go up and greet the crowd."

"No, I'm not going to do that. I don't even really want to sit on the platform. I'll just sit out front."

"I want you to sit by me," I repeated.

Ali reached out and put his arms around me and pulled me into one of the most loving, meaningful embraces that anyone has ever given me.

"You should be a spokesman for Jesus," I said. "Be a witness for Jesus."

He just looked at me and smiled as I got into the car.

I continued to pray for Muhammad Ali for the rest of his life, and I wish I could know what transpired in his mind and in his heart after our conversation. I do know that he wanted people of faith to get along and treat one another with love and respect. And I know he did not become the Muslim evangelist that others had hoped he would. He did not accept the offer to travel like the president in his own 747. I can only hope that God touched him at the end of his life and that the most famous man in the world finally met the greatest man to ever walk the earth, Jesus Christ.[3]

Hope Springs Eternal

Twenty-plus years ago, we were going to the ends of the earth with our ministry at LIFE Outreach. We were in Romania during the revolution; we were in Chernobyl during the aftermath of the nuclear disaster there; we were in Angola and Mozambique in the middle of the wars in those countries; we were in Rwanda during the genocide of the Tutsis; we were in Ethiopia at the height of the food crisis; and we were in Sudan when people were being killed everywhere and we would fly in under the radar with Franklin Graham.

We were also in China when the one-child policy was strongly enforced and babies, primarily girls, were being aborted at a sickening rate. Also, millions of children were housed in state orphanages in often appalling conditions. Untreatable diseases sometimes spread through the orphanages, and the healthy children would have to be separated from the sick ones, only to eventually watch their fellow orphans die. We were one of the few allowed to take our cameras into what were called the dying rooms—often just a bare floor where little children and babies were kept while they were dying.

We went into the dying rooms to pray for the babies who were scattered on the hard wooden floor, with no heat or air-conditioning, and we went out to the playgrounds to play with the other children at the schools associated with the orphanages. Around the cities, we saw babies in cardboard boxes, abandoned on the street, and it was more than a heart could take.

At one point, after we had been working there for years, we got permission from the Chinese authorities to put a Christian nurse or doctor into the orphanages where we were working. We also wanted to get air-conditioning and heat into the orphanages and make sure they had better food and medical supplies. But then because of some things that some other people did—we had nothing to do with it—the government reacted and cut everybody off. I think they also realized how fast the church in China was growing and were threatened by it. So they shut down foreign access to the orphanages.

They did, however, allow us to provide all the orphanages with illustrated children's New Testaments, in Chinese, because we asked permission of the local leadership and we had demonstrated the love of God to them over several years. One of the leaders said, through an interpreter, "These people love us. They're not just Western money-minded capitalists. They actually love us. So we're going to work with them." And we had indescribable access until the government shut it down.

One day I was walking down the hall in one of the orphanages, and I looked into a classroom with a mix of kids who appeared to be six to eight years old. I noticed one girl in particular, who was wearing a child-size Chinese military jacket, like she was in the army. As I stood at the door and watched her, I realized she was blind.

I walked over and knelt down in front of her. She put her tiny hands on my face and started feeling my features, rubbing her fingers around my eyes and touching my hair. I was there with a camera crew, so the camera was rolling right over my shoulder and capturing the look on her face.

She had reached out to me with such affection that I looked at her and said, "Honey, I know you can't see me, but I sure do love you. I want you to have hope, and I'm praying that somebody in America right now will see you on our television program and will give you a home."

In twenty-five years of active television ministry and all my travels throughout the world—seventy countries—we've never had a camera glitch. But right in the middle of my conversation with that little girl, the camera glitched, and it was visible on the film. The footage was blemished just enough that it was not up to our standards, and normally we wouldn't have used such a piece. But I had just told the little girl that I was praying that somebody in America would see her on the program and give her a home. So I said, "We *have* to use it."

Now here's where the story becomes miraculous. According to the rules in place at the time, a blind child could not be taken out of the country. On top of that, she had hepatitis B, and the American authorities wouldn't let her in to the country. Nevertheless, when we broadcast the story on our program, God spoke to a woman in Michigan who'd had three unsuccessful pregnancies in sixteen years of marriage, and told her, "This is going to be your daughter."[4]

So Brenda and Matthew Springstead worked out the details and went to China to adopt that seven-year-old blind girl with hepatitis. Her name was Hope. I think somebody told me that when I was at the orphanage, and I think that's why I said to her, "I want you to have hope."

When the Springsteads got off the plane with their new daughter, it seemed as if the entire town of Wyandotte, Michigan, was there to greet them. So many people had gathered you would have thought a planeload of soldiers was returning. And when they saw Hope for the first time, they all cheered.

After Hope had been in America for a year or two, we brought the whole family onto our television program and prayed for God to heal her. A doctor who heard her story called up and said, "I think I can correct her eyes."

Within a few years, the doctor performed the surgery and Hope's ability to see lights and shapes improved, but her vision was still not normal. Nevertheless, she overcame her disability, graduated from high school, and enrolled at Michigan State University.

During her senior year of college, she experienced a setback when she had an accident and lost nearly all the remaining vision in her right eye. Today, she still has some light perception with her left eye, but that too is diminishing.

In May 2010, Hope graduated from Michigan State with a degree in journalism, and she hopes to one day become the first blind anchorwoman on television. With her determination and perseverance, she has been an unbelievable inspiration and Christian witness.

But I can't forget to tell the rest of the story.

After Hope came to America, she kept telling her new parents that she had a friend who was still in China. We had seen this girl at the orphanage—her name is Kate—and she was a stick of dynamite.

Hope said, "I wish she could come over here."

So the Springsteads adopted Kate and brought her home, and Hope's friend became her sister. We had both girls on our show when they were still young, and Kate was so full of life and love that she just took over the program. Knowing where she had come from, and the circumstances surrounding her adoption, everyone in the studio that day was emotional.

Kate graduated from college several years ago and is now married with two children. Both she and Hope remain strong witnesses for the Lord.

In the years since the Springsteads adopted Hope and Kate, LIFE Outreach has helped to put a stop to the corruption and graft in the overseas adoption system. We have also helped to open up the process to make it easier for American families to adopt children overseas.

Even today I can see the fruit of our efforts firsthand as three of our staff members have adopted Chinese daughters into their families.

And that's why I continue to live amazed.

What the Bible Says about
LIVING AMAZED

At this point His disciples came, and they were amazed that He had been speaking with a woman.

John 4:27

All the people saw him walking and praising God . . . and they were filled with wonder and amazement at what had happened to him.

Acts 3:9–10

13

How *You* Can Begin to Live Amazed

When Jesus heard this, he was amazed and said to those following him, "Truly I tell you, I have not found anyone in Israel with such great faith."

Matthew 8:10 NIV

GROWING UP IN AUSTIN, Texas, I was a fatherless kid who had no clue what a father should look like. But now I know. I know my heavenly Father is indescribably wonderful—loving, patient, and kind—and He wants to show the world what He looks like and who He is. If people see the Father when they see the Son, as Jesus told Philip (see John 14:9), and if the church is the body of Christ, then people should see the Father when they see us.[1]

If I had listened to the people around me when I was growing up, I would have believed that God couldn't use someone like me. But God knew better. If I had allowed fear to guide me, I wouldn't have been able to speak to millions. But God had other plans. God led me into His purpose for my life, and because I followed Him, I have been living amazed ever since.

If you can get excited about what God has done with someone like *me*—someone who had every reason in life to fail—and if you can get excited about the greatness of the God who made all these things happen, I'm confident you can begin to see, understand, and get excited about how God can use *you*, right where you are, to touch the lives of other people in amazing ways.

If I can help you plug in to the power source—and stay plugged in—together we can inspire a nation and a generation to live amazed. If you will surrender your life to God, there's no limit to what He can do through you. "I tell you the truth," Jesus said, "anyone who believes in me will do the same works I have done, and even greater works, because I am going to be with the Father . . . so that the Son can bring glory to the Father."[2] This promise has yet to be fully realized, but it should inspire us to plug in to the Holy Spirit, who is the only One who can make it all happen.

> God can use you, right where you are, to touch the lives of other people in amazing ways.

New Eyes

I want to help you open your eyes to see God's love, purpose, and character all around you. I want to help you look through the eyes of Jesus and identify with the heart of God.

In my daily life, I don't look for opportunities; I look for God. I just walk the path and miracles happen. That's how I've learned to live, and it never stops. I can walk outside and give you several sermons in five minutes, just by observing the hand of God in nature. I can't look at dirt and not see God— I'm amazed by what we're able to do with dirt. Think about it: You have sand in your cell phone. That's why it works. If we look around and see life through God's eyes, we will behold His glory everywhere.

Consider something I've wondered about while looking around. If dirt could talk, what would it say? Perhaps it would ask sincerely, "Can I possibly grow something beautiful? Something really useful? Can I bear great and important fruit or food to nourish someone?" *Yes, you can!* Remember, we were created from the dust of the earth, and every one of us can grow something wonderful, beautiful, and meaningful.

It's amazing how God reveals himself in the world He created. However, we've become so twisted in our thinking, so programmed by the prevailing culture of skepticism, doubt, and deception that we can't get our spiritual eyes open. I want to help you refocus your vision so you can begin to see the hand of God in your life; so you can see all of life from a different perspective—God's perspective.

> In every situation— whether at home, at work, at school, or out in the community—look for evidence of God's hand, God's purpose, and God's character.

We need to have our vision *restored* and *refocused*. We need to be able to see life and people and our circumstances from God's point of view. Here's a simple way to start: In every situation—whether at home, at work, at school, or out in the community—look for evidence of God's hand, God's purpose, and God's character. Get in the habit of asking yourself a series of God-centered questions:

What does God want me to see?
What does God want me to share?
What does God want me to do?
How does God want me to respond?

Learn to respond to and obey God's still, small voice. Accept His leadership, trusting Him to produce the response and the results. We aren't called to be super salespeople. We are commissioned as witnesses for Christ, sharing His love and our own personal testimony. No testimony is insignificant. All are special and meaningful.

The more sensitive we are to what God sees, thinks, and feels, the more open we will be to having Him work through us—and the more amazing works we will see and be a part of.

> We are His workmanship, created in Christ Jesus for good works, which God prepared beforehand so that we would walk in them.[3]

But if we're caught up and absorbed in ourselves and our own issues, we won't see as clearly what God wants to do. Learn to say, "Lord, refocus my vision. Let me see what You see when You look out."

That's how my preaching ministry got started. I was sitting in a classroom at East Texas Baptist College, looking at all the other students in the room, and while they were listening to the professor—and I was *trying* to—I was asking God, *How do I reach him? How do I reach her? How could I talk to him? Her. That one. That basketball player. That popular student. That person who looks sad.*

God told me what to do, and I did what He said. And when I stood up in a coliseum or a stadium packed with thousands of people, I talked to them the same way God talked to me. But from a purely human perspective, it didn't make any sense that I was able to talk to them at all. Not considering where I had come from.

Living amazed is an ongoing, daily reality. If you will cease striving and know that God is God and start listening to what He says and seeing things differently—seeing things from God's perspective, with God's heart and compassion—not only will God be exalted among the nations and exalted in the earth, but He will also transform your life by renewing your mind and making your witness highly effective.[4]

Though I never graduated from East Texas Baptist College, I'll always be grateful for the honorary doctor of divinity degree they awarded me. I was overwhelmed by their recognition of my life's work. Let me share a truly amazing, supernatural experience that happened while I was a student there.

While I was attending the college, Betty and I lived outside the city limits in a small mobile home park that had one other unit besides ours. With our daughter Rhonda, who was three years old at the time, we called a ten-by-fifty-foot trailer home (yes, it was only ten feet wide). It's hard to imagine now, but that's where we lived.

People at the school were aware of my crusade ministry, and I had also been honored by the student body with two MVP awards in intramural sports after leading my football and basketball teams to undefeated seasons. As a result, I had gained some respect among the school's athletes.

East Texas Baptist had a very good basketball team, with an exceptional freshman player who excited everyone. I remember one game in which he made two free throws after time had expired to win the game by one point. I was so impressed by his composure under such tremendous pressure that I went to his dormitory later that evening to congratulate him. He wasn't there.

Around midnight, Betty and I were asleep in our trailer when someone started banging on our door. When I went to answer, I found the star freshman basketball player staring up at me.

"Come on in," I said. "Is everything okay?"

"Someone told me you knocked on my door," he said, "and I couldn't get to sleep without finding out why. I thought, *What does God want that James would come by to see me?* I just had to find out."

I told him why I had stopped by his room and also asked him about his relationship with Jesus. And in the wee hours of the night, while seated at the table in our little mobile home, he gave His life to Christ. I was overwhelmed with gratitude and joy.

That's what it's like to live amazed.

I hope you understand by now that God longs to bless you and to bless through you. If the only reason I wrote this book was so that God could bless you through it and you could learn to bless others, that's reason enough for me. I'm still on the journey right along with you. And I want to continue to grow while I'm trying to help others learn what it means to live amazed.

Small Is Beautiful

The Bible describes the church as the body of Christ—a body made up of many individual members, each with a vital role to play. For the body to function properly, each and every member must submit themselves to the head, who "makes the whole body fit together perfectly. As each part does its own special work, it helps the other parts grow, so that the whole body is healthy and growing and full of love."[5]

The three smallest bones in the human body are the middle ear ossicles—the malleus, incus, and stapes—more commonly known as the hammer, anvil, and stirrup. "The hammer is arranged so that one end is attached to the eardrum, while the other end forms a lever-like hinge with the anvil. The opposite end of the anvil is fused with the stirrup (so anvil and stirrup act as one bone)."[6]

That description of bones that are fused together makes me think of God's design for marriage, where two distinct lives are united to function as one. It's also one more example of the powerful hand of God at work, scattering images of His creative genius everywhere in the world for us to uncover. Part of living amazed is that we begin to see God's hand and heart and purpose in even the most mundane aspects of our lives.

Though the middle ear ossicles work in obscurity, completely invisible to the outside world, they are absolutely essential to our ability to hear. Without them, only 0.1 percent of the sound energy that hits the eardrum would be transferred to the inner ear.[7] But because God has arranged these tiny parts in a way that maximizes their leverage, they produce a sonic effect far beyond their diminutive size.

That too is a picture of God's creative genius—and His power. Like the feeding of the five thousand with five loaves and two fish,[8] God takes our yielded lives and multiplies the volume to accomplish His great purpose in the world.

Just as the human body has no insignificant parts, the body of Christ has no small or unimportant members. We all have a sphere of influence—however large or small, however visible or invisible—and we all have a vital role to play in God's plan for redeeming and restoring the world. We may be as well hidden as a bone in the inner ear, an internal organ, or a foot inside a shoe, but every person is absolutely essential to the eternal purpose of God. If every person in every church in every city could see—and truly grasp—that there are no small or insignificant members in the body of Christ, we would all be living amazed and the world would marvel.

Once we get excited about our role in God's kingdom and begin to realize the dreams God has for us—not just our own dreams—then we will begin to see the fulfillment of God's hopes and dreams for His body and His kingdom.

If you will surrender your life to God's kingdom—for His honor, His glory, and His purpose—you will find your own purpose. If you will give up your life to God, you will receive it back in abundance. When you discover the life God desires for you and the hopes He has for you, *your* hopes and dreams will be amazingly fulfilled in accordance with His will.

If you were to ask me one of the main keys to living amazed, I would say this: when Jesus says, "Whoever loses their life for my sake will find it,"[9] take Him at His word. Right from the start, Betty and I totally sold out to God's kingdom purpose, and whenever we've been distracted, deceived, or defeated, we have always sought diligently to return wholeheartedly to that commitment.

Noticing and Caring

One simple way you can start living amazed is by noticing people and caring about them. It's unbelievable what a difference it can make in people's lives.

John and Lisa Bevere are dear friends and two of the most highly visible speakers at conferences all over the United States, Australia, and Great Britain. Not long ago, Lisa reminded me about a citywide conference in Orlando I had spoken at after God set me free.

Before it was my turn to speak, I went to the makeup room to get ready, since cameras would be recording the conference. A young, dark-haired woman was doing the makeup, and though I didn't know it at the time, she had only one eye, having lost the other eye to cancer as a child. That makeup artist was Lisa Bevere. I'll let her tell the rest of the story.

> James, you looked at me not as a makeup person, but simply as a person, and you told me I was special to God, and that God was going to do something with me, and that I was going to be a tremendous blessing. I didn't have a father who ever loved me, so when you looked at me—someone you barely knew—and told me how special I was to God, it changed my life forever.
>
> Later in the week, my husband, John, came into the makeup room while you were there, and you looked over at him—and you didn't know he had just left a church as youth director, and that he was really hurt and disillusioned and didn't know what he was going to do—and you spoke into his life. You didn't know it, but you were speaking prophetically to him, and loving him, and the things you said to him changed his life.

Sitting there in that makeup room, more than twenty years ago, James, God used you, just caring about us, to change our lives. And God gave us a wonderful ministry, and four beautiful boys, and we have never been the same.[10]

I've known the Beveres for more than two decades, and I did not know the effect I'd had on their lives until recently, when Lisa told me this story. But it all came about because of one person noticing another and speaking simple words of life.

Anyone can do that. You can do that. And if you are willing to do that, there's no telling what God will do through you.

Investing in People's Lives

Sometimes the key to living amazed is making a simple investment in someone who just needs an opportunity.

Back when I was still doing the eight-day, Sunday to Sunday, citywide crusades, we realized we needed some help with public relations, communications, and our television ministry. We also needed someone who would be a good emcee on the platform and at the banquets where we did fund-raising for the crusades.

Someone told us about a gifted student named Mike Huckabee at Southwestern Baptist Theological Seminary, which is not far from our ministry offices. Mike had done a lot of radio and was a good communicator. So even though he was only twenty-one years old and still in his first year of seminary, we offered him a job. What was surprising was that his professors encouraged him to leave seminary early to go to work for us because they thought it was a great opportunity for him to work in our evangelistic outreach. Robert Naylor, the seminary's president, also encouraged Mike to take the offer.

When Mike came to work for us, he had a joyful spirit and a superb ability to communicate, but I noticed that he didn't seem to own a dress jacket. One day, I said, "Hey, Mike, come with me," and I drove him to the nicest department store in the mid-cities area and bought him three new suits with matching shirts and ties.

Mike was so excited, and so grateful, that I don't think there's any way I could have felt any more joyful about making those purchases. When you look at a small gesture like that and see the tremendous impact it can have on someone's life, it truly is amazing.

Mike worked with us for four years, and the last thing he did was set up the National Affairs Briefing, where Ronald Reagan won over the crowd. I think that's where Mike first recognized the importance of a strong Christian witness and the church having a positive and profound impact on the culture. And he has never forgotten that.

Mike, of course, went on to become governor of Arkansas, a Republican presidential candidate, and now a contributor on the Fox News Channel. In my opinion, he continues to be one of the great statesmen and witnesses for Christ today.

"Lord, I'm Not Worthy"

Throughout my journey, I have found it easy to agree with what the apostle Paul said about himself: "I am the foremost" among sinners.[11] Even after more than fifty years of public ministry, and almost sixty years of knowing Christ in a personal relationship, I can feel as unworthy as anyone I know.

So how can I begin to show you how to live amazed when I know so well the cracks in my own clay? Looking back at my journey and all the times I felt I had let down the Lord, never once did I feel that my heavenly Father was disappointed in me. Not once. No matter how miserably I failed or how inappropriate my words or actions were, God has never made me feel as if He's disappointed in me. He has compassion for me; He knows my frame; He knows that I am but dust;[12] and He knows how much I desire to serve Him. When things don't go well, He has always made me feel that He is disappointed *for* me, not *in* me.

God has always been the perfect Father, and He tells me what I need to hear. I remember clearly a time about thirty-five years ago when I was completely exhausted, feeling as if I had missed the mark, that I wasn't pleasing the Lord, and that I was undeserving of His name. I was sitting alone in a boat on a lake, fishing for bass and looking at the beauty of what God had created all around me. In what I thought was a voice of humility, I said, "Lord, I'm not worthy."

God's response was instantaneous, and I heard it with the force of a megaphone: "You never have been worthy, James. You never will be worthy. Worthy is the Lamb. I want you to preach and proclaim Him."

God's words hit me like a ton of bricks, but they also set my feet firmly on the path He wanted me to walk.

Even Jesus said, "The Son can do nothing of Himself, unless it is something He sees the Father doing; for whatever the Father does, these things the Son also does in like manner,"[13] and "The words that I say to you I do not speak on My own initiative, but the Father abiding in Me does His works."[14] We simply seek to do what Jesus did.

The enemy wants to magnify everything *except* Jesus. But if we are truly born of the Spirit and live by the Word, we will recognize the things of the Spirit and see the truth in God's Word. And the Spirit will always point us to Jesus—to His character, His mission, and His purpose.

One way we can see the amazing filling of the Holy Spirit in our lives is when He produces fruit that is contrary to our nature. Most people have some basic, natural, positive character traits. Some are laid-back—they seem calm and at peace when everything else is in turmoil—and others seem happy no matter what, they just have that demeanor by nature. But when someone like me, who can be combative, confrontational, and forceful, suddenly becomes kind and gentle, it can only be attributed to the *supernatural* work of God. When someone with an explosive temper suddenly finds self-control, or a person with no patience can be at peace while standing in line or stuck in a traffic jam, that's the signature work of the Holy Spirit.

When we live Spirit-filled lives—that is, under the control of the Holy Spirit—we are amazed to see how, even in our weakness, He is made strong. And we become free to surrender our gifts and strengths to the Spirit so that they too can be carried and controlled by Him.

Sadly, many people who go to church have never had an authentic encounter with the Holy Spirit. The enemy is clever about distracting, deceiving, and defeating us, so that we begin to think that such an encounter isn't possible or even desirable. But I don't believe the changes that have occurred in my life and the things the Lord has done with me are in any way unique. I believe God desires to change all of us more than we can even imagine. The changes I have seen in my life are infinitesimal compared to the changes God wants to bring to His church. You won't meet anyone on earth more anxious or aware of the need for change than I am, because I really do want to be conformed to the image of Jesus Christ.

I'm not interested in being a leader in the ways we often think of leadership. I want to learn what it means to be a servant and to serve other people. I want to see the body of Christ built up so that the church can do the work of ministry that God intends. And that means we must learn how to serve one another.

It's not about me. It's about God. We don't earn our value or merit God's blessings. But God loves to pour living water onto a dry and thirsty land. He will grow beautiful fruit in any yielded soil, any yielded life, as is evident in Isaiah 43:18–19:

Do not call to mind the former things, or ponder things of the past. Behold, I will do something new, now it will spring forth; will you not be aware of it? I will even make a roadway in the wilderness, rivers in the desert.

I want the story of my life to be the story of Christ's life in me. When God told me, in no uncertain terms, to proclaim the worthiness of Jesus, I realized that it's never about the greatness of an individual—even one who, by the world's standards, may be used in what appears to be an indescribably effective manner. It is always about God's greatness, God's grace, and God's power. God uses any available life, not because of the worthiness of the individual, but because of the beauty, power, and perfection of the One who seeks to live out His life through them.

> I want the story of my life to be the story of Christ's life in me.

The Journey Is the Goal

I believe we *all* have been invited to journey with Christ. God chose me. He also chose you. Will he put you on the same path he's put me on? Likely not. But I believe everyone has the potential to witness the things I have witnessed. I don't say this to compare your successes, failures, weaknesses, and strengths with mine. I simply mean that the Lord can and will do amazing things through your life, just as he has done through mine. As John Wimber told me years ago, "The journey is the goal." It's the pilgrim's progress. And we have no need to compare ourselves to one another.

It matters very little how I might be evaluated by you or by any human authority. I don't even trust my own judgment on this point. My conscience is clear, but that doesn't prove I'm right. It is the Lord himself who will examine me and decide.

So don't make judgments about anyone ahead of time—before the Lord returns. For he will bring our darkest secrets to light and will reveal our private motives. Then God will give to each one whatever praise is due.[15]

I hope this book has inspired you to realize that God can do mighty things with your life to accomplish His purpose and plan. I've shown you some of the supernatural ways He has worked in *my* life and in the lives of others I have known, and I hope you have seen in these divine encounters what it can mean for you if you listen to God when He speaks through the people He puts in your path. You may be surprised to see how powerfully God can use others to lead you to your purpose and help you fulfill it. That's part of what it means to live amazed.

Amazement is the result of seeing what God can accomplish through ordinary people. When he takes the clay of our lives and begins to shape vessels of honor, we become conduits for the free-flowing river of God's life and love. I don't mean *giftedness*, I mean *sensitivity* and *availability*—what I call *yieldedness* to the work of the Holy Spirit. We are uniquely created individual members of the body of Christ. Unique in every aspect of our being. We are here as a chosen generation, a royal priesthood, as witnesses and ambassadors for Christ. That's our purpose.

But let's make it personal: Once you understand why you're here, and once you begin to notice how God has gifted and placed you—that is, where God has you right now and the gifts He has given you right now—you will begin to see opportunities to be a conduit, a channel for His love and His purpose.

It takes faith the size of a mustard seed.[16] It takes the widow's mite or the last bit of oil and flour.[17] It takes five dinner rolls and two sardines.[18] It takes whatever we have to offer back to

God. From an eternal perspective, the things we might think are insignificant may have the greatest impact.

When I look back at my life, I realize that nothing could ever separate me from the love and grace of God. And I recognize that all greatness, and everything of real value, comes from God, comes through God, and is for God, as Jesus lives out His resurrected life through me and through everyone who will surrender to Him.

Even when we have walked away or turned our backs on God, He has never left us. He is always faithful. Like the father of the prodigal son, He's always ready and always waiting for us to come home.

In our day, it seems difficult for some people to even know where home is or what the Father looks like. And that's sad. But if the church will begin to live amazed, people will be able to see the Father who welcomes home every prodigal and adopts every fatherless orphan and gives them a home and a purpose that exceeds anything they could ever imagine.

One of the great joys of the past twenty-five years has been experiencing what you and every reader of this book can also experience. Rather than looking at how I can become a great preacher, teacher, leader, or whatever, I've learned to ask, *How can I become a truly yielded servant?* How can I become great in God's kingdom by having a servant's heart and wanting the best that God has for everyone?

We need *vision* to see things from God's point of view.

Open our eyes, Lord.

We need to surround ourselves with people who will point things out to us, so we can see the glory and love of God all around us.

Open our eyes, Lord.

We, as conduits of His grace and mercy, need to express the love of God to everyone we meet. We need to encourage others and be encouraged by others.

Lord, how can we reach the people who need encouragement? Make us sensitive to what You are doing all around us. Refocus our vision. Help us to see what You see when You look out. Help us to tend to Your sheep and not be invested in being noticed ourselves. Work through our lives, Lord, to show people that living amazed can be a daily, ongoing reality.

As the apostle Paul wrote to the churches in Rome and Corinth:

One of the things I always pray for is the opportunity, God willing, to come at last to see you. For I long to visit you so I can bring you some spiritual gift that will help you grow strong in the Lord. When we get together, I want to encourage you in your faith, but I also want to be encouraged by yours.[19]

Such confidence we have through Christ toward God. Not that we are adequate in ourselves to consider anything as coming from ourselves, but our adequacy is from God, who also made us adequate as servants of a new covenant, not of the letter but of the Spirit; for the letter kills, but the Spirit gives life.[20]

But we have this treasure in earthen vessels, so that the surpassing greatness of the power will be of God and not from ourselves; we are afflicted in every way, but not crushed; perplexed, but not despairing; persecuted, but not forsaken; struck down, but not destroyed; always carrying about in the body the dying of Jesus, so that the life of Jesus also may be manifested in our body. For we who live are constantly being delivered over to death for Jesus' sake, so that the life of Jesus also may be manifested in our mortal flesh. So death works in us, but life in you.[21]

Turning toward the Light

Some time ago, my friend Foster Friess and I were sitting together on a dam overlooking a twelve-acre lake. As we were enjoying the scenery, I asked him, "Can I tell you what I see when I look out over this landscape?"

"Sure," he answered.

"I'm looking at the trees, the flowers, the grass, and every plant, and I see them all reaching up as high as they can toward the light. Every blade of grass, every leaf, every flower, is seeking and turning toward the light, following the sun as it rises and sets.

"And I'm the same way myself; I can't get enough light. I'm looking at nature's law and nature's God. I'm looking at the ultimate Creator. And everything I look at is seeking the light.

"Did you know that when the sun comes out from behind the clouds, many flowers open up? And at the same time that every leaf, every flower, and every blade of grass is turning toward the light, their roots are going down as far as they can into the soil to get the water and nutrients that are essential for growth.

"God says, 'I have revealed myself in everything I have created. Look at it. It's all reaching for the light. It always turns to the light. And it's reaching down for water.'

"And God says, 'The only part of my creation that *doesn't* consistently do that are the *people* I created in My own image. They don't faithfully turn to the light. They don't look to the light while reaching down for the water of My Word. And they're not being rooted and grounded in love.' How sad!"

I looked over at Foster at this point, and there were tears rolling off his cheek.

"Do you see how God is speaking to us in everything He created?" I asked. "Everywhere I look, I behold His glory. And when the Son stands out and I see His radiance, just as with the flowers and the trees I bear fruit."

That's why I live amazed in the light of God's love and the water of His Word. And you can begin living amazed right now as you yield your life to the fullness of God's Spirit, losing your life to His will and His kingdom purpose.

Index of Amazing Bible Verses

Notes

Chapter 1 Miracle in Marble Falls

1. See the Index of Amazing Bible Verse, on page 213.
2. Mark 9:15; 10:32.
3. John 14:12 NLT.
4. See Acts 3:1–15; 4:5–14; 8:9–24; 9:20–22; 10:44–48; 12:11–17; 13:8–12.
5. Italics added.

Chapter 2 Plucked from Obscurity

1. 1 Samuel 13:14; Acts 13:22.
2. See Judges 6 and 7.
3. Judges 7:12.

Chapter 3 Answering the Call

1. 2 Timothy 2:16.
2. 2 Timothy 2:23.
3. Romans 12:1–2 KJV.
4. Philippians 2:5–11 KJV.
5. 1 Corinthians 2:1–5 KJV.
6. Matthew 10:18–20 KJV.
7. Though the original of this letter has been lost, the text was printed as an endorsement on the back flap of the dust jacket on one of my early books, *America: Garden of the Gods and Other Messages* (Atlanta: Cross Roads Publications, 1976).
8. It was common during the early days of my evangelistic ministry for pastors of churches where we held our meetings to write letters of

recommendation to other pastors in the denomination. These endorsements helped us secure future opportunities for ministry. This letter, from April 1963, came to me from O. C. Robinson, but it was also sent out to other Southern Baptist Convention pastors.

9. Romans 8:28.

Chapter 4 Burnout

1. Frank H. Harber, "An Examination of the Historical Development of the Ministry of the Evangelist within the Christian Church" (PhD diss., Southwestern Baptist Theological Seminary, 1994).

2. Isaiah 65:2.

3. See Revelation 2:1–7.

4. See Judges 16:21.

5. John 10:27.

6. 1 Chronicles 21:1.

7. 1 Chronicles 21:3.

8. Isaiah 43:19 NLT.

9. See Philippians 3:13–14.

Chapter 5 God's Amazing Unity

1. Vance Havner, interview with Dennis Hester in "Vance Havner: Enjoying the Desires of His Heart," *Proclaim*, October 1982, http://vancehavner .com/vh-enjoying-the-desires-of-his-heart-2.

2. See 1 Corinthians 3:1–4.

3. 1 Corinthians 3:4.

4. 1 Corinthians 3:6.

5. 1 Corinthians 3:1 NIV.

6. Galatians 5:22–23.

7. Galatians 5:19–21.

8. Matthew 5:14.

Chapter 6 God's Amazing Healing

1. John 14:12.

2. John 3:11–12.

3. Matthew 13:54.

4. Matthew 13:58.

5. Jaine Treadwell, "Kim Lunsford's Life Had Impact on Community," *Troy Messenger*, June 21, 2000, www.troymessenger.com/2000/06/21/kim -lunsfords-life-had.

6. See Matthew 19:15; Mark 5:23; 6:5; 8:23; 10:16; 16:18; Luke 4:40; 13:13; Acts 6:6; 8:17–19; 9:12–17; 13:3; 19:6; 28:8; 1 Timothy 4:14; 2 Timothy 1:6.

Chapter 7 God's Amazing Heart for the Lost

1. Peter Jenkins, *A Walk Across America* (New York: Morrow, 1979), 248–49.
2. Ibid., 260–61.
3. Skip Hollandsworth, "Blood Will Sell," *Texas Monthly*, March 2000, www .texasmonthly.com/articles/blood-will-sell.
4. 1 Samuel 16:7 NLT.
5. See, for example, Matthew 23:1–33.
6. Luke 18:10–14.
7. Mary Jimenez, "Evangelist Brings His Message to Youths," *Shreveport Times*, October 12, 2006, www.gotellministries.com/posts/all/ministries/crusades /page/4.
8. Lisa Rice, "Crusade Evangelism? Still Works for Rick Gage," *SBC Life* (February 2007), www.sbclife.net/Articles/2007/02/sla14.

Chapter 8 God's Amazing Provision

1. Nehemiah 9:26.
2. Matthew 6:33 ESV.
3. 1 Kings 17:8–16.
4. Luke 4:25–26.
5. Luke 4:27.
6. John 4:10, 14 NLT.
7. John 4:29–30 NLT.
8. John 4:32, 34.
9. John 4:35–36.
10. 2 Corinthians 12:9.

Chapter 9 God's Amazing Hand on History

1. Associated Press, "Televangelist Rex Humbard Dies at 88," The Christian Broadcasting Network, www.cbn.com/spirituallife/churchandministry /clergy/humbard.aspx?mobile=false.
2. "James Robison: National Affairs Briefing (James Robison/LIFE Today)," YouTube video, 12:57, from the National Affairs Briefing in Dallas, TX, on August 20, 1980, posted by *LIFE Today*, March 31, 2014, www.youtube.com /watch?v=lH1eOxxRRbk.
3. Ibid., 5:20.
4. Ibid., 14:24.
5. Jerry Naylor, conversation with the author, April 27, 2016.
6. Melinda Rose, "A History of the Laser: A Trip through the Light Fantastic," *Photonics Spectra*, May 2010, www.photonics.com/Article.aspx?AID =42279.

Chapter 10 God's Amazing Hand on His Church

1. John 14:6.
2. Matthew 5:14–16.
3. Ronald Reagan, "Farewell Address to the Nation," January 11, 1989, The American Presidency Project, University of California, Santa Barbara, www.presidency.ucsb.edu/ws/?pid=29650.
4. See Nehemiah 2:17–4:23; 6:15–16.
5. Abraham Lincoln, Second Inaugural Address, March 4, 1865, The Avalon Project, Yale Law School, http://avalon.law.yale.edu/19th_century /lincoln2.asp.
6. Ibid.
7. 1 John 4:18.
8. Romans 8:37 ESV.
9. 2 Corinthians 3:17 ESV.
10. 1 John 4:1.
11. 1 Peter 1:22.
12. James 5:16, author's paraphrase of the KJV.
13. John 16:8.
14. Jude 20–21 NLT.
15. Jude 22–23 NLT.
16. "Father Raniero Cantalamessa," accessed August 8, 2016, www.canta lamessa.org/?page_id=201&lang=en.
17. Rick Warren, *The Purpose Driven Life*, ex. ed. (Grand Rapids: Zondervan, 2012), 23.
18. "(Un)Qualified Steven Furtick Retailer Video Message," YouTube Video, posted by Mardel Christian & Education, January 20, 2016, www.you tube.com/watch?v=5UveKxMmtgI.
19. John 17:20–21.

Chapter 11 A Life Filled with Amazing Encounters

1. See Ephesians 6:10–18.
2. Matthew 25:40.
3. 1 Peter 1:8.

Chapter 12 God's Amazing Work in the World

1. John 17:20–21.
2. *The Apostle*. Written and directed by Robert Duvall. October Films, 1997.
3. Adapted from James Robison, "My Amazing Encounter with Muhammad Ali," *The Stream*, June 5, 2016, https://stream.org/james-robison-my -amazing-encounter-with-muhammad-ali/.

4. Some of the details in this account are from Jim Kasuba, "Wyandotte: Gaining Independence—Lion's Club Gives Blind Woman GPS (with video)," *The News Herald,* January 31, 2011, www.thenewsherald.com/articles/2011/01/31/news/doc4d430f55090108133312619.txt?viewmode=fullstory.

Chapter 13 How *You* Can Begin to Live Amazed

1. Romans 12:4–5; 1 Corinthians 12:12–13, 27.
2. John 14:12–13 NLT.
3. Ephesians 2:10.
4. Psalm 46:10; Romans 12:2.
5. Ephesians 4:16 NLT.
6. Douglas E. Vetter, "How Do the Hammer, Anvil, and Stirrup Bones Amplify Sound into the Inner Ear?" *Scientific American,* January 31, 2008, www.scientificamerican.com/article/experts-how-do-the-hammer-anvil-a.
7. Ibid.
8. Matthew 14:13–21.
9. Matthew 10:39.
10. Lisa Bevere, conversation with the author, May 17, 2016.
11. 1 Timothy 1:15 ESV.
12. Psalm 103:13–14.
13. John 5:19.
14. John 14:10.
15. 1 Corinthians 4:3–5 NLT.
16. Matthew 17:20.
17. Mark 12:41–44; 1 Kings 17:8–16.
18. John 6:4–14.
19. Romans 1:10–12 NLT.
20. 2 Corinthians 3:4–6.
21. 2 Corinthians 4:7–12.

James Robison is the founder and president of LIFE Outreach International and host of the daily television program *LIFE Today*. He has spoken to more than twenty million people through hundreds of citywide evangelistic outreaches and has personally inspired religious, political, and social leaders for five decades. He has dedicated his life to such ministry work as feeding people in crisis situations, drilling water wells, establishing orphanages and schools, building homes for the homeless, and rescuing women and children from sex trafficking. In 2015, James launched a new website called The Stream (stream.org) that presents breaking news, editorial commentary, inspiration, and cultural analysis. He is the author of the *New York Times* bestselling book *Indivisible*, as well as numerous other books. He lives in Fort Worth, Texas, with his wife, Betty. For more information, visit www.lifetoday.org.

LIFE TODAY online anytime.

Stay connected with *LIFE TODAY* . . .

a daily outreach of ministry, inspiration, and encouragement
hosted by James and Betty Robison. Here you will find real
stories of life, challenges, victories, and faith in times of crisis.
You can also stay updated on mission outreaches from around
the world. And with social media and mobile platforms,
LIFE is available literally *anytime* and *anywhere*.

LIFETODAY.ORG

James & Betty Robison

LIFE OUTREACH INTERNATIONAL